THE BULLET POINT
LEADER
UNLOCK YOUR TRUE POTENTIAL

TERENCE E. MURPHY

THE BULLET POINT LEADER

Unlock Your True Potential

"If you don't know what port you're sailing to, no wind is favourable".

- Seneca

CONTENTS

FORWARD

Dear Reader,

In a world overflowing with leadership wisdom, self-help gurus, and endless theories, it's easy to get lost in the noise. We often find ourselves drowning in a sea of advice, struggling to discern what truly matters in the realm of leadership. It's at moments like these that we crave a straightforward compass, a no-nonsense guide, a roadmap that cuts through the fluff and nonsense and gets to the heart of the matter.

I stand before you today as someone who's trodden this path for over four and a half decades, right in the heart of London—a city that's as diverse, vibrant, and unpredictable as life itself. My journey hasn't been paved with gold, nor have I had the privilege of a perfect upbringing or an assembly line of role models. Instead, I've relied on my trusty "Spidey senses" to navigate the challenges and opportunities that life in this bustling metropolis presents.

I've read more leadership books than I can count—over forty, to be precise. Some were riveting, some were, well, less so. I've coached countless individuals, each with their unique aspirations and stumbling blocks. I've lived a life, seen my fair share of highs and lows, and cherished the role of a devoted husband and father to two wonderful children. I am also acutely aware of my failings in these two most important roles. I also studied as a coach and cognitive therapist and various other "people related" pursuits.

Through it all, I've remained a staunch believer in the power of helping people discover and pursue their goals. I've witnessed the transformation that occurs when individuals tap into their potential, find their inner compass, and chart their course towards success. And that's what this book is all about.

This isn't your typical cover-to-cover read. It's not a lecture filled with complex theories and endless anecdotes. Instead, it's a toolkit, a collection of insights, a series of navigational beacons to help you find your way through the maze of leadership.

You can pick it up, open it anywhere, and find a nugget of wisdom that speaks to your current journey. You can skip chapters that don't resonate with you, return to others when the time is right, and flip through the pages like a menu, selecting what suits your palate.

Throughout these (bullet points) chapters, you'll find a blend of my experiences, the distilled wisdom from those forty-plus books. It's a no-frills, matter-of-fact guide that aims to demystify leadership and make it accessible to all.

Whether you're an aspiring leader, a seasoned executive, or someone simply seeking inspiration, this book is for you. It's a companion for the curious, a reference for the determined, and a reminder that leadership isn't reserved for a chosen few—it's a journey we all embark upon, whether we realise it or not. YOU ARE A LEADER.

So, as you delve into these pages, remember that leadership isn't just about titles, corner offices, or grand speeches. It's about understanding yourself, connecting with others, and making a positive impact in your own unique way. It's about embracing your Spidey senses, trusting your inner compass, and navigating the bustling streets of life with confidence.

I invite you to explore, reflect, and apply the insights you discover here. Let this book be your trusty guide, your practical companion, and your source of clarity in the world of leadership. With each chapter, you'll inch closer to unlocking your leadership potential and forging your own path to success.

So, without further ado, let's embark on this journey—because, in the end, leadership is not a destination; it's a continuous, ever-evolving adventure. And I'm excited to share it with you.

I bet you could go through it in a couple of hours.

With simplicity and sincerity,

Terry x

Just a heads up before you start reading.

- › There are no perfect leaders.
- › The grammar will surely be pants.
- › I rinsed the thesaurus option to death and learnt some new words in the process.
- › I used quillbot to proofread the text.
- › Some leaders DO NOT deserve the title. You know who they are. They don't.
- › It will most certainly be repetitive. (For this I DO NOT apologise). Discipline requires repetition.
- › This is a piece of work based on my life in business thus far.

» You or any reference to you are not featured in this book.

» If you role your eyes when some leaders are talking, this is natural.

» Never stop believing.

» Always get back up again.

» I wasn't 100% sure on the colour of the cover, so I checked it with Jade.

» The cover is Blue.

» I haven't completed a reference list; I've used the name/surname of the authors. I quote from the book list at the end. I may miss some.

» You are a leader. Sometimes you need to hear it more than once.

» Enjoy

Unleashing the Power of Leadership

The role of a leader is more than just a position; it is a profound responsibility that shapes the destiny of an organisation. It is a journey that demands clarity of purpose, an unwavering belief in the team, and a commitment to excellence. This journey of leadership is not a mere job; it's a calling, a vocation that echoes the motivational fervour and insightful wisdom often associated with business thought leaders like Simon Sinek and Tony Robbins.

The Visionary Trailblazer

A leader isn't merely a manager; they are a visionary trailblazer. They possess the remarkable ability to see beyond the horizon, to envision a future that is not constrained by the present. Just as Sinek famously emphasises the importance of "starting with why," leaders begin with a purpose. They understand that leadership is about guiding the team towards a shared vision, inspiring them to rally behind a cause that is greater than themselves.

Coaching for Peak Performance

Effective leaders understand that leadership is not about commanding, but about coaching. They recognise that their team members are not just employees but individuals with unique talents and potential waiting to be unlocked. They invest time and effort in coaching their team, nurturing their growth, and helping them achieve peak performance. It's not just about managing tasks; it's about developing people.

Mastering the Art of Communication

Communication is the lifeblood of effective leadership. Adept leaders master the art of communication, understanding that clarity and transparency are essential. They can articulate their vision, expectations, and feedback with precision and persuasiveness. They listen attentively, not only to what is said but also to what remains unsaid. They comprehend that, as Robbins often says, "The quality of your communication determines the quality of your leadership."

Adaptability in a Shifting Landscape

The business world is dynamic, constantly evolving. Leaders must be adaptable and resilient, capable of navigating through the turbulence of change. In line with the teachings of Robbins, they see adversity as an opportunity for growth. They understand that resilience is the cornerstone of leadership, allowing them to lead their teams through uncertain terrain with unwavering determination.

Building an Empowered Team and Culture

Creating a thriving departmental culture is akin to crafting a masterpiece. Leaders are the artists, setting the tone for an environment where teamwork, innovation, and excellence flourish. Just as Sinek emphasises the importance of trust and cooperation within an organisation, leaders understand that culture is not just about rules; it's about shared values and behaviours that drive success.

Fostering Innovation and Embracing Risk

Innovation and calculated risk-taking are essential components of leadership. Leaders encourage their teams to step outside their comfort zones, to challenge the status quo, and to embrace change. They recognise that, as Robbins famously asserts, "The only limit to your impact is your imagination and commitment." They inspire their teams to push boundaries, to think creatively, and to innovate relentlessly.

The Human-Centric Approach

Leaders are not just managers of resources; they are stewards of people. They embody empathy, recognising the inherent humanity in every team member. In the words of our guiding lights, "The quality of your leadership is the quality of your relationships." This holds true in the realm of leadership. Leaders who genuinely care for their team members build bonds that are unbreakable.

Strategic Prowess

In a world awash with data and information, the ability to make strategic decisions is paramount. Leaders possess the acumen to set clear goals, develop actionable plans, and steer their teams towards success. They understand that strategic thinking is the compass that guides them through the labyrinth of business challenges.

A Commitment to Lifelong Learning

Great leaders are perpetual students of their craft. They recognise that leadership is an ever-evolving journey of continuous improvement. Just as Sinek and Robbins advocate for lifelong learning, leaders invest in their own growth and the development of their teams.

THE TAKEAWAY: Unleash the Power Within

In the world of leadership, the power to transform, inspire, and achieve is within reach. It's not about titles or positions; it's about the lives we touch, the visions we inspire, and the legacy we leave. When leaders embrace their roles with clarity, purpose, and an unwavering belief in their teams, they become catalysts for excellence. They illuminate the path to success in the grand symphony of business, leaving an indelible mark on the organisations they serve.

....

Core Principles

In the world of business, leadership isn't just a role; it's a profound responsibility that transcends titles and positions. Effective leadership is about setting a strong foundation built upon core principles that inspire and guide not just the leader but the entire team towards success. In this exploration, we will delve into the essence of effective leadership, embracing the motivational fervour and insightful wisdom often associated with business thought leaders.

The Essence of Leadership

Leadership isn't about authority; it's about influence. It's about inspiring others to voluntarily follow a shared vision and purpose. Just as Sinek urges us to "start with why," effective leaders begin by defining the 'why' that drives their actions and the actions of their teams. This 'why' is the moral compass that guides their decisions and inspires their teams to greatness.

Integrity and Authenticity

The foundation of effective leadership is built upon a bedrock of integrity and authenticity. Leaders who walk the talk, who exemplify the values they espouse, are the ones who earn the trust and respect of their teams. Authentic leaders don't put on masks; they are genuine, transparent, and consistent in their words and actions.

Empathy and Emotional Intelligence

To lead effectively, one must understand and connect with the human dimension. Empathy, as Robbins often emphasises, is the ability to put oneself in another's shoes, to truly understand their thoughts and feelings. Effective leaders possess high emotional intelligence, enabling them to relate to the struggles, aspirations, and concerns of their team members.

Communication and Active Listening

Communication is the lifeblood of leadership. Effective leaders excel not only in conveying their vision but also in actively listening to their team members. They create an open and inclusive environment where everyone's voice is heard and valued. As Sinek would say, "Great leaders are willing to sacrifice their own interests for the good of the group."

Vision and Purpose

A compelling vision and a sense of purpose are the driving forces behind effective leadership. Leaders articulate a clear vision that paints a picture of a better future, inspiring their teams to journey towards it. Purpose gives meaning to the work, transforming it from mere tasks into a shared mission that fuels motivation and commitment.

Accountability and Responsibility

Effective leaders understand that accountability starts at the top. They take responsibility for their actions and decisions, setting an example for their teams. They create a culture of accountability where individuals take ownership of their work and its outcomes. As Robbins says, "The only thing that's keeping you from getting what you want is the story you keep telling yourself."

Adaptability and Resilience

The business world is marked by constant change and unpredictability. Effective leaders are adaptable and resilient, capable of navigating through challenging times with grace and determination. They embrace change as an opportunity for growth and innovation, echoing Robbins' belief that "Life is a gift, and it offers us the privilege, opportunity, and responsibility to give something back."

Empowerment and Trust

Leadership isn't about micromanagement; it's about empowerment. Effective leaders trust their teams to make decisions and take calculated risks. They provide guidance and support, allowing team members to grow and develop their skills. Trust is the cornerstone of a high-performing team, as Sinek would remind us, "When people are financially invested, they want a return. When they are emotionally invested, they want to contribute."

Conflict Resolution and Collaboration

During any leadership journey, conflicts are inevitable. Effective leaders possess the skill to navigate through conflicts constructively, fostering resolution and collaboration. They create an environment where diverse perspectives are welcomed, recognising that innovation often emerges from the clash of ideas.

Continuous Learning and Personal Growth

Just as Sinek and Robbins advocate for lifelong learning, effective leaders are perpetual students of their craft. They invest in their own growth, constantly seeking to enhance their leadership skills and knowledge. They understand that leadership is an ongoing journey of self-improvement.

THE TAKEAWAY: The Bedrock of Excellence

The foundation of effective leadership is a potent blend of integrity, authenticity, empathy, and communication. It's about inspiring a shared vision and fostering a culture of accountability, empowerment, and continuous learning. As leaders embrace these core principles, they not only guide their teams towards success but also leave an enduring legacy of excellence. In the grand tapestry of leadership, these principles serve as the solid ground upon which leaders build a brighter future for themselves and their organisations.

Before we move on, I think there's a relevance to the work I've been reading over the last four months. I was introduced to the stoics by Ryan Holiday after finding a podcast that featured him. His passion was captivating and something that I warmed to immediately. I entered that mystical world of the past, littered with wisdom and truth. I've always been on a quest to find straightforward, no-nonsense approaches and this certainly deserved my attention. My journey took an unexpected turn when I stumbled upon the Stoics, particularly Marcus Aurelius and his book, "Meditations."

I began my leadership journey like many others, eager to uncover the secrets of effective leadership. I looked to contemporary leadership experts and bestsellers, hoping to find the keys to success. However, it was during this chance encounter that I discovered a book that would change my perspective.

"Mediations" by Marcus Aurelius wasn't your typical leadership guide. It was a collection of personal reflections by a Roman emperor, written during times of immense external pressure. What struck me was that this ancient wisdom was not only timeless but surprisingly relevant to the modern world of leadership. We must remember, these were the personal thoughts of Caesar. They were for his eyes only.

What appealed to me most about the Stoics, and Marcus Aurelius in particular, was their emphasis on self-mastery. They believed that leadership begins with mastering oneself—controlling your impulses, emotions, and responses to external events. This made sense to me because I had seen many leaders stumble not because of external challenges but due to their own lack of self-control.

My journey into Stoicism was practical. It demanded introspection and a willingness to confront my own flaws and biases. It wasn't about adopting a new set of rules but about gaining a deeper understanding of myself and the world around me.

One key takeaway from the Stoics was the idea of distinguishing between what's within your control and what's not—an essential principle. This shift in perspective enabled me to focus my energy and efforts on things I could influence, leading to more effective decision-making and a reduced sense of frustration when faced with uncontrollable external forces.

Reading "Meditations" exposed me to Marcus Aurelius' remarkable ability to find strength in adversity. His concept of "amor fati," or love of fate, encouraged me to view setbacks as opportunities for growth and resilience. This Stoic mindset has become a cornerstone of my leadership philosophy, enabling me to lead with grace even in turbulent times.

Incorporating Stoicism into my leadership journey is transformative in a practical sense. It has allowed me to lead with greater authenticity, humility, and empathy. I learned that leadership isn't about being perfect but about striving for virtue, even when the going gets tough.

As you move through these pages on your own leadership journey, consider exploring Stoicism. It may not offer all the answers, but it certainly provides practical insights that can guide you towards becoming a more effective and grounded leader.

Let's move on.

Lessons from Successful Leaders

Crafting a visionary culture isn't just a goal; it's a necessity. It's the bedrock upon which thriving organisations are built. While drawing inspiration from renowned thought leaders like Simon Sinek and Tony Robbins, we explore the principles that underpin visionary cultures and the wisdom that successful leaders have woven into their fabric.

The Genesis of Visionary Culture

A visionary culture isn't an overnight creation but a deliberate, evolutionary process. It commences with leaders who possess a profound sense of purpose and an unwavering vision for their organisations. These leaders are like architects, drafting a blueprint for the culture they aspire to instil.

The Role of Purpose

Purpose stands as the beating heart of any visionary culture. Leaders grasp the significance of a compelling 'why' – a magnetic force that draws individuals towards a shared mission. They communicate this purpose with crystalline clarity, breathing life into it and instilling a sense of meaning in the hearts of their team members.

Alignment with Values

To build a visionary culture, leaders must align their organisations with a set of core values that mirror their mission and beliefs. These values serve as the guiding principles governing actions and decisions throughout the organisation. They're not mere words on a wall but living, breathing standards that shape behaviours.

Leadership by Example

Leaders who inspire visionary cultures aren't just orators; they lead by example. Authenticity reigns supreme, as they mirror the values and principles they champion. Through their actions, they set the tone, showing their teams what it means to embody the culture they're striving to create.

Empowerment and Trust

Empowerment and trust are bedrock principles in a visionary culture. Leaders place their faith in their teams, empowering them to make decisions and take ownership of their work. They provide support and guidance while allowing room for innovation and exploration. Trust is the cornerstone upon which a culture of excellence is erected.

Clear Communication

Communication fuels the engine of a visionary culture. Leaders communicate their vision and values with transparency and consistency. They cultivate an atmosphere of open dialogue where ideas are welcomed, and questions encouraged. A shared vision thrives in an environment of free exchange.

Adaptability and Continuous Learning

A visionary culture is dynamic, not stagnant. Leaders cultivate a culture of continuous learning and growth, embracing change as an opportunity for improvement. They instil a mindset of innovation and agility, echoing the idea that life offers us the privilege to give something back through our commitment and imagination.

Recognition and Celebration

Successful leaders understand the significance of recognising and celebrating achievements. They acknowledge team contributions, reinforcing the culture's values. Celebrations become moments of shared triumph, enhancing the sense of belonging and pride within the organisation.

Diversity and Inclusion

In visionary cultures, diversity of thought, background, and perspective is celebrated. Leaders recognise that innovation flourishes where different viewpoints collide. They foster an inclusive culture where every voice is heard, and everyone feels valued and included.

Resilience and Adaptation

A visionary culture isn't impervious to challenges. It thrives in adversity. Leaders instil resilience in their teams, guiding them through difficult times with determination and grace. They understand that the capacity to adapt and endure is key to impact.

Long-Term Perspective

Building a visionary culture requires patience and a long-term view. Leaders invest in the growth and development of their team members, understanding that a sustainable visionary culture rests on a foundation of continuous improvement.

THE TAKEAWAY: The Legacy of Visionary Culture

A visionary culture is the thread weaving together individuals, values, and purpose. It's the enduring legacy of leaders who have harnessed the wisdom of visionaries, creating environments where greatness flourishes. As leaders embrace these lessons and nurture visionary cultures, they guide their teams towards success and leave a legacy of purpose, values, and innovation. They inspire others to do the same, creating a ripple effect that extends far beyond the boundaries of their organisations.

Let's pause again before you move on.

The concept of vulnerability has emerged as a cornerstone of authenticity and connection. Brene Brown, a prominent researcher and author, has played a pivotal role in reshaping how we perceive vulnerability, and her insights have influenced my journey.

Brown's assertion that "Vulnerability is not winning or losing; it's having the courage to show up and be seen when we have no control over the outcome" encapsulates the essence of vulnerability. It's not about weakness; rather, it's about having the courage to be our true selves, even when it feels uncomfortable. Marcus Aurelius anybody?

Society often reinforces the idea that displaying vulnerability is a sign of weakness. Yet, through Brene Brown's research and teachings, we see that vulnerability is a wellspring of strength and human connection.

In the realm of leadership, the pressure to appear invulnerable can be overwhelming. We often wear a mask of strength and infallibility, believing that leaders should never show signs of uncertainty or doubt. Brown's work challenged this notion, asserting that authentic leadership necessitates vulnerability.

As I reflect on my own journey, I can trace the transformation that vulnerability has wrought in my approach. It dawned on me that genuine leadership stems from deep, human connections, which are only possible when we embrace vulnerability as a path to authenticity.

Vulnerability doesn't entail revealing every detail of our lives. Rather, it involves being honest about our thoughts, feelings, and fears when they impact our work and relationships. It means having the courage to admit when we don't have all the answers, seeking assistance when necessary, and receiving feedback with humility. I can't remember who said it, but "transparency with wisdom" comes to mind.

She underlines the role of leaders in shaping the culture of their teams and institutions. By demonstrating vulnerability, we set the tone for our teams to follow suit.

Now, let's explore how vulnerability dovetails with the idea of a visionary culture. A visionary culture is one that encourages bold thinking, innovation, and a shared sense of purpose. It's a culture that rallies individuals around a compelling vision of the future.

In this context, vulnerability serves as the foundation upon which a visionary culture can thrive. When leaders and team members alike embrace vulnerability, it creates an environment where radical ideas can be openly discussed without fear of judgment. It encourages individuals to share their dreams, even if they appear audacious or unconventional.

I'm not advocating that boardrooms or staff meetings become a feelings fest, but more a place of openness and greater depth.

Within a visionary culture, leaders who exhibit vulnerability become catalysts for transformation. Their willingness to admit uncertainties and seek input from their teams fosters a sense of collective ownership over the vision. This, in turn, fuels innovation as team members feel empowered to propose novel solutions and challenge the status quo.

In such an environment, vulnerability acts as a bridge between visionary aspirations and practical implementation. It invites discussions about the risks and obstacles associated with the vision, allowing teams to develop contingency plans and navigate potential pitfalls more effectively.

Furthermore, vulnerability within a visionary culture promotes inclusivity. When team members know that their voices are valued, regardless of their position or tenure, it encourages diversity of thought and perspectives. This diversity, in turn, enhances the robustness of the vision by considering a broader range of possibilities and challenges.

Brene Brown's exploration of vulnerability has indelibly shaped my perspective on leadership and personal growth. Vulnerability is not synonymous with weakness but a manifestation of courage. It's the courage to be authentic, to forge meaningful connections, and to lead with empathy and humility.

Within the context of a visionary culture, vulnerability takes on a new dimension. It becomes the connective tissue that bridges visionary aspirations with pragmatic execution. It empowers team members to contribute their boldest ideas, fostering innovation and inclusivity along the way. As Brene Brown aptly says, "Vulnerability is the birthplace of love, belonging, joy, courage, empathy, and creativity." Embracing vulnerability, alongside a visionary culture, is the path to creating a more compassionate, resilient, and innovative organisation.

Coaching's up next. I do love coaching. ☺

COACHING FOR SUCCESS

....

Strategies and Techniques

Coaching isn't merely an option; it's a strategic imperative. It's the turbocharge that propels individuals and teams towards peak performance and unparalleled success. In this pivotal chapter, we dive headfirst into the dynamic realm of coaching, infused with impactful strategies and techniques that are the linchpin of transformation, not just in business but in life itself.

The Art and Science of Coaching

Coaching is a finely honed craft that blends the art of inspiration with the science of human behaviour. At its core, coaching is about illuminating the path to success, shedding light on the latent potential that resides within everyone.

The Power of Vision

Effective coaching starts by kindling the spark of vision. It's about digging deep to uncover the 'why' behind individual goals. A compelling vision is the fuel that propels individuals forward, igniting their passion and commitment. Coaches guide individuals to unearth their core purpose, aligning their actions with this magnetic force.

Active Listening and Empathy

Coaches master the art of active listening, tuning in not just to words but to emotions, aspirations, and the unspoken. Empathy reigns supreme; it's the bridge that connects coach and individual, creating an environment of trust and understanding.

Goals as North Stars

Coaching is goal-centric, with objectives as guiding stars. Coaches work side by side with individuals to craft crystal-clear, specific goals. These aren't vague wishes; they're tangible targets that act as lighthouses, cutting through the fog of uncertainty.

Constructive Feedback as Fuel

Coaches are adept at offering insights and perspectives that help individuals see their blind spots and areas for improvement. It's not criticism; it's a gift that propels individuals towards excellence. Feedback is a compass pointing to the path of continuous improvement.

Accountability and Responsibility

Coaches hold individuals accountable for their actions and commitments. It's not about control; it's about empowerment. Coaches instil a sense of responsibility, fostering the understanding that success ultimately lies in one's hands.

The Power of Visualisation

Coaches encourage individuals to vividly picture their success. This mental rehearsal enhances belief and resilience, anchoring the vision of achievement deep within the subconscious.

Collaborative Journey

Coaching isn't a one-way street; it's a dynamic, collaborative journey. Coaches recognise that individuals are the experts of their lives. Coaches tap into the well of wisdom within everyone, helping them draw out solutions and strategies.

Leveraging Strengths

Effective coaching often leverages strengths. Coaches identify an individual's natural talents and abilities and find ways to amplify and apply them. This strengths-based approach fosters confidence, competence, and a sense of achievement.

Reflecting on Progress

Coaching isn't a one-off intervention; it's an ongoing, dynamic process. Coaches guide individuals in reflecting on their progress, celebrating their victories, and learning from their setbacks.

Resilience and Grit

In the face of challenges, coaching instils resilience and grit. Coaches help individuals develop the mental and emotional fortitude to persevere when the road gets tough.

Personalised Strategies

Individuals are unique, and so are the strategies and techniques employed by coaches. Coaches tailor their approach to meet the specific needs and circumstances of everyone. It's not a one-size-fits-all solution; it's a customised roadmap to success.

THE TAKEAWAY: Coaching as the Catalyst for Achievement

Coaching is not just a set of strategies and techniques; it's the ignition that sets the spark of potential ablaze. It's the journey of empowerment, growth, and self-discovery. It's about unlocking the full spectrum of human capabilities, propelling individuals and teams towards excellence. Effective coaching is the driving force behind personal and professional transformation. It's the art of sculpting success stories, one coaching session at a time, and paving the way for individuals to stride confidently towards their desired futures, ready to conquer any challenge and achieve their most ambitious dreams.

As I am a staunch advocate for coaching and I like to dig a little deeper, I had to go on a long and dusty journey of discovery many years ago. Stick with me on this one as we delve into The Bible.

The Bible, an ancient and revered text, is often viewed through the lens of religion and spirituality. Yet, beyond its spiritual significance, I've come to appreciate it as a wellspring of coaching wisdom. As I delve into its pages, I see a remarkable guide for personal growth, leadership, and coaching.

Consider the story of Moses. When he led the Israelites out of Egypt, he faced a formidable task of guiding a vast multitude through the wilderness to the Promised Land. In many ways, Moses embodied the essence of a coach. He listened to the concerns of his people, provided direction, and motivated them to overcome obstacles.

Moses's journey reflects the coaching process of transformation. He navigated resistance, facilitated learning, and encouraged his followers to embrace change. His unwavering commitment to their growth parallels the role of a coach in fostering personal and professional development.

King Solomon, renowned for his wisdom, is another biblical figure whose teachings hold valuable coaching insights. His famous decision to resolve the dispute between two women claiming the same child demonstrates the importance of active listening and discernment in coaching.

In coaching, active listening is the cornerstone of understanding and assisting clients. Solomon's wisdom encourages us to dig deeper, asking probing questions to uncover underlying issues and helping clients make informed choices.

The story of David and Goliath is a testament to courage and resilience in the face of overwhelming odds. David, a young shepherd, confronted the giant Goliath with nothing but a slingshot. His unwavering faith in his abilities and his willingness to take risks exemplify coaching principles.

Coaches often help clients confront their "Goliaths"—daunting challenges and fears. David's triumph teaches us that with the right mindset and support, individuals can overcome seemingly insurmountable obstacles.

Jesus used parables to convey profound life lessons. These stories resonate with coaching techniques, as they encourage introspection and self-discovery. Consider the Parable of the Prodigal Son, which explores themes of forgiveness, redemption, and personal growth.

Coaches often use storytelling to help clients gain insights and explore their own narratives. The parables of Jesus serve as powerful examples of how storytelling can facilitate self-reflection and transformation.

The letters of the Apostle Paul to early Christian communities are filled with words of encouragement, guidance, and motivation. His role as a spiritual mentor aligns with the coaching practice of providing support and empowerment.

In coaching, encouragement is a vital tool for helping clients build confidence and resilience. Paul's letters remind us of the impact of positive reinforcement in guiding individuals toward their goals.

The Bible, though primarily a spiritual guide, offers a rich tapestry of coaching wisdom. Through the lives of biblical figures and the teachings of Jesus and others, we find lessons in leadership, transformation, resilience, and empowerment.

As a coach, I've discovered that the Bible can serve as a timeless and universal source of guidance. Its stories and principles resonate with coaching practices and offer profound insights into the human experience.

Just as Moses led his people to the Promised Land, coaches guide their clients towards their desired destinations. Like Solomon's wisdom, coaching involves careful listening and discernment. The courage of David and the storytelling of Jesus inspire us to help clients face challenges and explore their stories.

Ultimately, the Bible can be seen as a coaching companion—a source of inspiration and wisdom that transcends time and culture. As we navigate the complexities of coaching, let us draw from the well of biblical insight to support and empower those we serve. Here endeth the lesson.

Let's move on.

THE ART OF COMMUNICATION

Leading with Clarity

Effective communication isn't just a skill; it's the backbone of success. It's the ability to convey ideas, inspire action, and build strong connections. In this chapter, we embark on a journey into the heart of communication, infused with the power and punchiness that is quintessentially British. Let's explore the art of communication, where clarity reigns supreme, and leaders wield words like master craftsmen, shaping the destiny of their organisations.

The Power of Clarity

At the heart of effective communication lies the jewel of clarity. It's the ability to express ideas, thoughts, and intentions in a manner that leaves no room for misunderstanding. Clear communication is the linchpin that keeps teams aligned, propels projects forward, and ensures that everyone is on the same page.

Stripping Away Ambiguity

Effective communication doesn't dabble in ambiguity; it thrives on precision. Leaders understand that vague or convoluted messages breed confusion and can lead to costly missteps. They strip away ambiguity, choosing words that leave no room for interpretation.

The Three Cs

Clarity, conciseness, and consistency are the golden trio of communication. Leaders embrace brevity, delivering messages in a concise manner that respects the value of everyone's time. They maintain consistency in their messaging, ensuring that the information shared aligns with the overarching goals and values of the organisation.

Listening as an Art

Communication isn't a one-way street; it's a dynamic exchange. Just as talking is crucial, listening is an art. Leaders practice active listening, giving full attention to the speaker, understanding not just the words but the emotions and intentions behind them.

Empathy in Communication

Effective leaders don't just speak; they connect. They infuse empathy into their communication, understanding the perspectives and feelings of their audience. They create an environment where individuals feel heard and valued.

Tailoring the Message

One size does not fit all in the world of communication. Leader's tailor their message to suit the audience. They consider the background, knowledge, and interests of the recipients, ensuring that the message resonates with them.

Storytelling as a Weapon

Stories are the secret weapon of communication. Leaders use storytelling to convey complex ideas, make concepts relatable, and ignite emotions. A well-told story can captivate, inspire, and drive action.

Visual Communication

In a world where attention spans are shorter than ever, visual communication is a potent tool. Leaders leverage visual elements such as charts, diagrams, and infographics to convey information in a compelling and easy-to-understand manner.

Feedback as a Two-Way Street

Communication isn't just about delivering messages; it's about fostering a culture of feedback. Leaders encourage open and honest feedback, both giving and receiving. They understand that feedback is a valuable resource for improvement and growth.

Transparency and Trust

Trust is the currency of effective communication. Leaders maintain transparency in their communications, sharing information openly and honestly. They understand that trust is fragile and that once broken, it's challenging to rebuild.

Overcoming Communication Barriers

Barriers to effective communication are ubiquitous. These can be cultural, linguistic, or even technological. Leaders take proactive steps to identify and overcome these barriers, ensuring that their message reaches its intended destination intact.

The Written Word

In a world flooded with written communication, leaders understand the power of the written word. They craft emails, reports, and documents with precision and clarity, recognising that written communication can leave a lasting impact.

Non-Verbal Communication

The unspoken also speaks volumes. Leaders are attuned to non-verbal cues, such as body language and facial expressions. They use their own non-verbal communication to reinforce their spoken message.

Crisis Communication

In times of crisis, effective communication becomes paramount. Leaders have a crisis communication plan in place, ensuring that they can respond swiftly and decisively to unforeseen challenges without compromising clarity or transparency.

Multichannel Communication

In a digital age, leaders harness the power of multichannel communication. They use a variety of platforms, from email to social media, to reach different segments of their audience effectively.

Empowering Others to Communicate

Leaders don't hold the monopoly on communication; they empower others to communicate effectively as well. They provide training and guidance, nurturing a culture where everyone is a communicator.

THE TAKEAWAY: The Clear Path to Leadership

The art of communication is the compass that guides leaders through uncharted waters. Clarity is the beacon that keeps teams united, stakeholders informed, and organisations on course. Effective communication is the cornerstone of successful leadership, a journey where words are wielded with precision and power, paving the way for leaders to navigate challenges, inspire action, and lead their organisations to resounding success.

Let's see how MLK Jr. did communication. Now I know a lot of leadership books quote MLK Jr. But "The Words of Martin Luther King" (Coretta Scott King) has been a companion that sits on my bedside table, and travels with me when I remember.

Martin Luther King Jr.'s unparalleled communication skills not only made him a civil rights icon but also offer profound lessons for effective leadership. As I've explored his work and reflected on his role in history, I've come to recognise how his communication abilities set a remarkable example for leaders in various domains. Here, I'll delve into how King's communication style can be a source of inspiration and guidance for leadership.

One of the most critical tasks is to inspire a shared vision. Martin Luther King Jr.'s "I Have a Dream" speech remains a prime example of how to articulate a compelling vision that rallies people behind a cause. His dream of a future free from racial discrimination was not just his; it became a shared vision that resonated with millions.

Leaders, too, must craft and communicate a vision that inspires others to join them on the journey. King's ability to paint a vivid picture of a better future, rooted in justice and equality, serves as a reminder that leaders should be visionary communicators who ignite passion and purpose among their teams.

Effective leaders are often skilled persuaders, and King's persuasive abilities were exceptional. His message was not confrontational but rooted in love, justice, and unity. He appealed to the moral and ethical conscience of the nation, emphasizing the shared values of equality and human dignity.

In leadership, persuasion is about more than convincing; it's about winning hearts and minds. King's approach teaches us that to lead effectively, we must appeal not only to reason but also to the values and emotions that connect us all.

Leadership often involves facing adversity and challenges, and King's life serves as a testament to resilience and courage. Despite threats, violence, and imprisonment, he remained steadfast in his commitment to nonviolence and justice. His resilience in the face of adversity is an inspiration for leaders navigating difficult situations.

In leadership, resilience is a valuable trait. Leaders must be prepared to persevere through setbacks, maintain their integrity, and remain committed to their values and mission. King's ability to lead with grace under duress reminds us that resilience and courage are essential qualities for effective leadership.

Leaders today operate in an increasingly globalized world, and King's global perspective is instructive. While his primary focus was on the civil rights struggle in the United States, his message of justice, equality, and nonviolence had global implications. His advocacy for nonviolence as a means of social change inspired movements for justice worldwide.

Leaders must recognise the interconnectedness of our world and the importance of addressing global issues. King's global outlook encourages leaders to consider the broader impact of their actions and decisions and to work towards a more just and equitable global society.

Martin Luther King Jr.'s communication style in contemporary leadership cannot be overstated. In a world grappling with complex challenges such as social inequality, climate change, and political polarization, his emphasis on nonviolence, unity, and empathy provides a powerful template for leaders.

His approach to leadership through communication challenges us to prioritize dialogue over confrontation, compassion over division, and justice over injustice. His enduring legacy reminds us that leaders can be effective catalysts for positive change when they lead with authenticity, vision, and a commitment to the betterment of society.

Martin Luther King Jr.'s exceptional communication skills make him not only a civil rights icon but also a model of communicative leadership. His ability to inspire a shared vision, persuade with love and justice, exhibit resilience, maintain a global perspective, and remain relevant in contemporary leadership all contribute to his enduring legacy.

As leaders, we can draw valuable insights from King's communication style and apply them to our own leadership journeys. We can strive to be visionary communicators, persuasive advocates for justice, resilient in the face of adversity, and global-minded leaders who inspire positive change.

Martin Luther King Jr. reminds us that effective leadership begins with effective communication, rooted in values that uplift humanity. His legacy challenges us to be leaders who not only lead organisations but also inspire movements, transform societies, and work towards a world where justice and equality prevail.

Whoop, good leaders have a mountain to climb. Let's never stop striving to communicate effectively.

Leadership Styles

Leadership is not a one-size-fits-all proposition. Each department, like a distinct instrument in an orchestra, demands its unique conductor, each with a style tailored to bring out the best in the team. As we journey through the diverse landscape of departmental leadership, we explore the dynamic styles that light the path for departmental leaders, carving the way for their teams' success.

The Symphony of Leadership Styles

Just as a conductor's baton dictates the tempo and mood of a musical piece, departmental leaders wield their leadership styles to set the tone and direction. Leadership is not just a position; it's an art, a fluid melody that adapts to the needs and dynamics of each department.

The Art of Autocratic Leadership

In some departments, a firm and guiding hand is essential. Autocratic leadership, akin to the conductor's precision, is about making decisions swiftly and with authority. Departmental leaders assert control, providing clear direction and expecting strict adherence to their guidance.

The Harmonious Democracy of Democratic Leadership

Other departments thrive on collaboration and shared decision-making. Democratic leadership is akin to a democratic conductor who seeks input from each section of the orchestra. Departmental leaders engage their team members in decision-making, valuing their contributions and fostering a sense of ownership.

Laissez-Faire Leadership: The Jazz of Departmental Leadership

I had to get French and Jazz in here somewhere. ☺

Some departments are like jazz ensembles, where creativity flows and improvisation reigns supreme. Laissez-faire leadership, like the freewheeling spirit of jazz, grants team members considerable autonomy. Departmental leaders offer guidance when needed but largely allow their team to chart their course.

The Steady Rhythm of Transformational Leadership

In departments facing challenges and change, transformational leadership takes the stage. These leaders are like conductors who inspire their orchestra to transcend limits. Departmental leaders set high expectations, encourage innovation, and lead by example, inspiring their teams to reach new heights.

The Supporting Role of Servant Leadership

Servant leaders are the behind-the-scenes conductors, focusing on the needs of their team members. Much like an orchestra's support staff, they work tirelessly to ensure their team can perform at their best. Departmental leaders in this style prioritise the development and well-being of their team members.

The Pragmatism of Transactional Leadership

In departments that demand order and structure, transactional leadership is the tune to follow. Leaders set clear expectations and reward or correct based on performance. It's akin to the conductor who ensures each note is played correctly, maintaining discipline and accountability.

The Agility of Situational Leadership

Situational leaders are like conductors who adapt to the changing mood of a piece. They assess each situation and adjust their leadership style accordingly. Departmental leaders in this style are flexible, recognising that what works for one project or challenge may not work for another.

The Transparent Leadership of Authenticity

Authentic leaders are like transparent conductors, revealing their genuine selves to their teams. They build trust by being open and honest, fostering an atmosphere where team members feel comfortable sharing their ideas and concerns. This style promotes genuine connections and cooperation.

Leading with Empathy

Regardless of the style, successful departmental leaders share a common thread: empathy. They understand the strengths and weaknesses of their team members and provide support where needed. They listen, offer guidance, and recognise the importance of maintaining a healthy work-life balance.

Departmental Dynamics

Each department within an organisation has its unique culture and needs. The role of the departmental leader is to understand and adapt to these dynamics. They must strike a delicate balance between aligning with the overall organisational goals and tailoring their leadership style to suit the specific challenges and opportunities within their department.

The Art of Blending Styles

Effective departmental leaders are often maestros who blend multiple leadership styles as the situation demands. Just as a conductor may use different techniques to guide an orchestra through various movements, departmental leaders combine styles to lead their teams through the ever-changing landscape of business.

Cultivating Future Leaders

In the world of departmental leadership, the baton must be passed. Successful leaders invest in the development of future leaders within their departments. They mentor and nurture talent, ensuring that the symphony of leadership continues to play in harmony, creating a legacy of success.

THE TAKEAWAY: Leading the Departmental Symphony

Departmental leadership is an intricate dance, a symphony where the conductor's style must harmonise with the orchestra's unique composition. Departmental leaders are not just managers; they are the conductors of success, guiding their teams with skill and adaptability. Each department may have its tune, but with a skilled leader at the helm, they all contribute to the grand symphony of organisational success.

Aligning Your Department's Mission

Leadership isn't merely about managing; it's about steering the ship towards a meaningful destination. Each department is like a compass, guided not just by objectives but by a deeper sense of purpose. In this chapter, we dive headfirst into the exhilarating world of purpose-driven leadership, let's explore how aligning your department's mission can be the key to unlocking exceptional results.

The North Star of Purpose

Purpose is not just a buzzword; it's the magnetic force that draws individuals and teams towards a shared mission. It's the "why" that gives meaning to the "what" and "how." Purpose-driven leadership begins by understanding and articulating why your department exists beyond the numbers and targets.

Transcending the Bottom Line

While financial success is undoubtedly vital, purpose-driven leadership goes beyond profit margins. It's about acknowledging the broader impact of your department's work on stakeholders, society, and the environment. It's the recognition that your department is a part of a larger ecosystem, and its actions ripple far and wide.

Inspiring a Shared Vision

A department's mission isn't just a statement; it's a vision that ignites passion and commitment. Effective leaders inspire their teams by aligning the department's mission with the personal aspirations and values of team members. They create a vision that resonates, fostering a sense of purpose that transcends the daily grind.

Mission as a Guiding Light

In the tumultuous waters of business, a clear mission acts as a guiding light. It provides direction when decisions are tough, and challenges seem insurmountable. Leaders use the department's mission as a touchstone, ensuring that every action and decision is in alignment with its core purpose.

The Ripple Effect of Alignment

Alignment with a department's mission doesn't just benefit the team; it extends to stakeholders, customers, and the organisation. When everyone is moving in sync towards a common purpose, it creates a ripple effect of positive outcomes.

Walking the Talk

Purpose-driven leaders don't just talk about the mission; they embody it. They lead by example, demonstrating through their actions that the department's mission isn't just lip service. They ensure that every decision, no matter how small, reflects the core values and purpose of the department.

The Power of Employee Engagement

Aligned with a purpose, employees are not just workers; they are champions of the mission. Purpose-driven leaders understand that engaged employees are more motivated, innovative, and committed. They invest in creating an environment where team members feel connected to the mission and understand their role in achieving it.

Cultivating a Culture of Purpose

Culture isn't just a buzzword either; it's the soil in which a department's purpose takes root and flourishes. Purpose-driven leaders nurture a culture where the mission is not just a poster on the wall but a way of life. They foster an atmosphere of shared values and a collective commitment to the greater purpose.

Purpose-Driven Decision-Making

In a world inundated with choices, purpose acts as a compass for decision-making. Purpose-driven leaders use the mission as a litmus test, ensuring that every choice aligns with the greater vision. This clarity simplifies decision-making and reduces the risk of straying off course.

Continuous Alignment

Purpose-driven leadership is not a one-time endeavour; it's an ongoing journey. Leaders recognise that as circumstances change, the department's mission may need adjustment. They are agile, ready to realign the mission when necessary, ensuring it remains relevant and inspiring.

Measuring Impact

Purpose-driven leadership isn't just about feel-good sentiments; it's about results. Leaders use key performance indicators (KPIs) to measure the impact of alignment with the mission. They track not only financial metrics but also social, environmental, and stakeholder indicators.

Communicating the Mission

Effective leaders are master communicators of the department's mission. They use clear and compelling language to convey the purpose to team members, stakeholders, and the broader community. They understand that effective communication reinforces alignment.

Leading with Ethics and Integrity

Purpose-driven leadership goes hand in hand with ethics and integrity. Leaders understand that the department's mission is best achieved through honest, ethical means. They set high standards of conduct, ensuring that every action reflects the values inherent in the mission.

Inspiring the Next Generation

Purpose-driven leaders understand the importance of legacy. They inspire the next generation of leaders by passing on not just the baton but the torch of purpose. They mentor and nurture emerging leaders, ensuring that the department's mission continues to guide future endeavours.

THE TAKEAWAY: Leading with Purpose

Leading with purpose isn't just about achieving success; it's about leaving a legacy. Purpose-driven leadership is the rudder that steers departments towards meaningful destinations, where every action and decision is in harmony with the greater mission. Effective leaders are not just managers; they are navigators, guiding their teams towards purpose and prosperity. They understand that purpose isn't a destination; it's the journey itself, one filled with passion, meaning, and a shared commitment to making a positive impact on the world.

Transforming Your Leadership Mindset

The transition from a manager to a leader is akin to shifting gears from driving a car to piloting an aircraft. It's not just a change in role; it's a profound shift in mindset and approach. In this chapter, we soar into the exhilarating world of leadership transformation, let's explore the journey of evolving from a manager into a true leader.

The Manager vs. Leader Distinction

Before we embark on the transformational journey, let's clarify the manager vs. leader distinction. Managers focus on processes, efficiency, and day-to-day tasks. Leaders, on the other hand, cast their gaze on the horizon, guiding the team towards a shared vision and purpose.

Embracing Vision

Leaders are navigators of the future. They understand that a compelling vision is the magnetic force that propels a team forward. Transforming from a manager to a leader begins with embracing and articulating a clear, inspiring vision that ignites passion and commitment.

Leading by Example

Leaders don't merely delegate tasks; they roll up their sleeves and lead by example. They understand that their actions speak louder than words. Transforming your leadership mindset means being a role model, demonstrating the qualities and values you expect from your team.

Empowering and Developing Talent

A manager often focuses on getting the job done, while a leader is committed to growing their team members. Transforming into a leader means shifting from a task-driven mindset to one that prioritises talent development and empowerment.

Effective Communication

Leaders are exceptional communicators. They excel not only in conveying ideas but in inspiring action and building strong connections. Transforming your leadership mindset involves honing your communication skills, from active listening to inspiring speeches.

Strategic Thinking

A manager operates within the framework of processes, while a leader thinks strategically. Leaders zoom out to see the bigger picture, understand market trends, and anticipate future challenges. Transforming into a leader means developing a strategic mindset that aligns actions with long-term goals.

Embracing Change

Change is a constant in the business world. Managers may resist change, focusing on maintaining stability. Leaders, however, embrace change as an opportunity for growth and innovation. Transforming your leadership mindset means becoming a change agent, guiding your team through transitions with confidence.

Risk-Taking and Innovation

Leaders are willing to take calculated risks in pursuit of innovation. They understand that failure is often a steppingstone to success. Transforming from a manager to a leader involves encouraging a culture of innovation, where team members feel safe to experiment and learn from setbacks.

Inspiring and Motivating

A manager may use rewards and punishments to motivate the team, but a leader inspires intrinsic motivation. Transforming into a leader means learning to tap into the unique aspirations and strengths of each team member, fuelling their passion and commitment.

Building Trust and Accountability

Leaders prioritise trust and accountability. They understand that trust is the foundation of a strong team. Transforming your leadership mindset means fostering an environment of trust where team members feel safe to speak their minds and take ownership of their actions.

Conflict Resolution

Conflict can be a roadblock to progress. Leaders are skilled mediators, resolving conflicts in a constructive manner. Transforming into a leader means developing conflict resolution skills, turning conflicts into opportunities for growth and collaboration.

Adapting to Feedback

Leaders are receptive to feedback, recognising it as a valuable resource for improvement. Transforming your leadership mindset involves a willingness to listen, learn, and adapt based on feedback from team members and stakeholders.

Staying Resilient

Leaders are pillars of resilience. They maintain composure and adaptability in the face of adversity. Transforming from a manager to a leader involves developing emotional intelligence and the ability to stay calm under pressure.

Mentoring and Developing Others

A leader's legacy is not just about personal success but about the success of those they mentor and develop. Transforming your leadership mindset means investing in the growth of others, passing on knowledge, and nurturing emerging leaders.

Embracing Humility

Leaders are humble. They recognise that leadership is a continuous journey of learning and growth. Transforming into a leader involves shedding ego and being open to different perspectives and ideas.

Leading with Purpose

Purpose is the compass that guides leaders. Transforming your leadership mindset means aligning your actions with a deeper sense of purpose that transcends the daily tasks. It's about understanding the "why" behind what you do and inspiring your team with this shared sense of mission.

THE TAKEAWAY: The Journey of Transformation

The transformation from manager to leader is not just a career progression; it's a profound personal and professional journey. It's about evolving from a taskmaster into an inspirational guide, from a process-oriented manager into a strategic thinker and visionary leader. Effective leaders are not just managers with a fancier title; they are the architects of success, the navigators of uncharted waters, and the torchbearers of a brighter future. It's a journey filled with challenges, learning, and growth, where the destination is not just success but a legacy of leadership excellence.

Adapting Your Department for the Future

Change isn't just a constant; it's a force that shapes the landscape and determines the fate of organisations. The ability to navigate change effectively can mean the difference between thriving and merely surviving. In this chapter, we plunge headfirst into the ever-evolving world of change management, let's explore how to adapt your department for the future and emerge not just unscathed but stronger and more resilient.

The Imperative of Change

Change isn't a matter of choice; it's a necessity. The business environment is in a state of perpetual flux, driven by technological advancements, shifting consumer preferences, and global events. The failure to adapt to change can leave a department obsolete and stagnant.

Embracing a Growth Mindset

Adapting to change begins with cultivating a growth mindset. Leaders and team members alike must be open to learning, unlearning, and relearning. A growth mindset is about seeing challenges as opportunities for growth and embracing change as a chance to innovate.

The Power of Anticipation

Change is often less disruptive when anticipated and planned for. Department leaders should be vigilant, keeping an eye on industry trends, emerging technologies, and potential disruptors. Proactive anticipation allows for more strategic and less reactionary responses to change.

Clear Communication

Effective communication is the linchpin of change management. Leaders must communicate the reasons for change, the expected outcomes, and the roles team members will play. Transparent and frequent communication fosters understanding and buy-in.

Engaging Stakeholders

Change doesn't happen in a vacuum. It affects not only internal team members but external stakeholders as well. Engaging with stakeholders, from customers to suppliers, is crucial. Their insights and feedback can inform the change process and lead to more successful outcomes.

Change Champions

Identifying and empowering change champions within the department can be transformative. These individuals are passionate advocates for change, rallying their colleagues and driving enthusiasm for new initiatives. They play a pivotal role in facilitating change adoption.

Data-Driven Decision Making

In an era of data abundance, decisions should be informed by data and evidence. Data-driven decision-making reduces uncertainty and enhances the likelihood of successful change. Departments should invest in data analytics and research to support their strategies.

Agile Adaptation

Change isn't always linear; it can be dynamic and unpredictable. Departments should adopt an agile approach, allowing for flexibility and quick adjustments as needed. Agile teams are more responsive to change and can seize opportunities more effectively.

Continuous Learning

Change is an opportunity for growth and development. Departments should invest in ongoing training and development for team members, equipping them with the skills and knowledge needed to thrive in a changing landscape.

Risk Management

Change inherently involves risks. Departments should conduct thorough risk assessments, identifying potential challenges and developing mitigation strategies. A well-thought-out risk management plan can reduce the impact of unforeseen obstacles.

Innovation and Creativity

Change often breeds innovation. Departments should foster a culture of creativity, where team members are encouraged to generate new ideas and solutions. Innovation can be a powerful driver of competitive advantage.

Resilience Building

Change can be challenging, and setbacks are a part of the process. Building resilience within the department helps team members bounce back from adversity. Leaders should provide support and resources for mental and emotional well-being.

Measuring and Evaluating Change

Change should not be a shot in the dark; it should be measured and evaluated. Departments should establish key performance indicators (KPIs) and benchmarks to assess the impact of change initiatives. Regular evaluations allow for course corrections.

Feedback Loops

Feedback is a valuable tool in the change management toolkit. Departments should create feedback loops that allow team members to share their experiences and insights. Feedback can reveal challenges and opportunities that might have been overlooked.

Celebrating Success

Amidst the challenges of change, it's important to celebrate successes, no matter how small. Recognising achievements and milestones boosts morale and reinforces the benefits of change.

Embracing Digital Transformation

In an increasingly digital world, departments must embrace digital transformation. This may involve adopting new technologies, automating processes, and leveraging data analytics. Digital transformation is often at the heart of remaining competitive and relevant.

Sustainability and Social Responsibility

Change isn't just about adapting to market forces; it's also about embracing sustainability and social responsibility. Departments should consider their environmental and social impacts, seeking ways to align with ethical and sustainable practices.

THE TAKEAWAY: Sailing into the Future

Change is the wind that fills the sails, propelling departments towards new horizons. Adapting for the future isn't an option; it's a mandate for survival and success. Effective change management is not a passive reaction; it's a proactive, strategic approach. It's the art of embracing change as an opportunity, a chance to innovate, grow, and thrive in the face of uncertainty. It's about steering the ship with purpose and resilience, navigating the waves of change, and emerging not just intact but stronger and more ready for the challenges that lie ahead.

Building High-Performing Teams

The quest for building high-performing teams has become the holy grail of success. Picture a team that not only meets but exceeds expectations, a group of individuals who synergise seamlessly, achieving remarkable results that leave the competition in awe. This chapter delves into the art of hiring and developing talent, unveiling the secrets to crafting teams that go beyond the ordinary.

The Talent Imperative

In the 21st century, talent is the new currency. It's not just about having a workforce; it's about having the right workforce. Hiring the right people can set your organisation on a trajectory of perpetual growth and innovation. But here's the secret sauce: it's not just about what they bring to the table today; it's about what they can become.

The Growth Mindset

To build high-performing teams, you must adopt a growth mindset. This concept, popularised by psychologist Carol Dweck, asserts that individuals who believe their abilities can be developed through hard work, learning, and persistence are more likely to succeed. When hiring, seek out candidates who embody this mindset. They are not afraid to tackle challenges head-on and view failures as opportunities to learn and grow.

The Power of Purpose

Purpose-driven individuals are the fuel that powers high-performing teams. When people believe in the mission and values of your organisation, they are more likely to invest their time and energy into making it a success. During the hiring process, probe candidates not only for their skills and experience but also for their alignment with your company's purpose.

Cultivating Potential

Once you've assembled your team of purpose-driven, growth-minded individuals, the real work begins. Developing talent is an ongoing journey, and it requires a commitment to nurturing their potential. Here's how:

Continuous Learning: Encourage a culture of continuous learning. Provide opportunities for team members to acquire new skills and knowledge, whether through workshops, courses, or mentorship programs.

Feedback Loop: Create a feedback-rich environment. Constructive feedback helps individuals understand their strengths and weaknesses, enabling them to grow and improve.

Empowerment: Trust your team members to make decisions and take ownership of their projects. Empowered individuals are more likely to innovate and excel.

Stretch Assignments: Challenge your team with stretch assignments that push them beyond their comfort zones. It's in these moments of discomfort that true growth occurs.

Diversity Drives Excellence

High-performing teams are often diverse teams. Diversity brings together different perspectives, ideas, and experiences, leading to more innovative solutions and better decision-making. Embrace diversity not as a checkbox but as an essential ingredient in your talent mix.

A Culture of Collaboration

The days of the lone genius are long gone. Building high-performing teams means fostering a culture of collaboration. Encourage open communication, teamwork, and the sharing of ideas. When individuals feel valued and heard, they are more likely to contribute their best work.

Leadership's Role

Leadership plays a pivotal role in talent development. Leaders should not only set the example but also create an environment where growth and innovation are celebrated. They should lead by empowering others, setting clear expectations, and providing the necessary resources for success.

Measuring Success

Finally, building high-performing teams requires the ability to measure success effectively. Look beyond traditional metrics like revenue and profit. Consider the satisfaction and engagement of your team members. Are they thriving and growing? Are they proud to be a part of your organisation?

Hiring and developing talent is an art that, when mastered, can transform your organisation into a powerhouse of innovation and success. Seek individuals who embody a growth mindset and align with your purpose. Nurture their potential through continuous learning, feedback, and empowerment. Embrace diversity, foster a culture of collaboration, and lead by example. Success will not be far behind as you unlock the full potential of your team, propelling your organisation to new heights.

Look at some of the questions you might ask when onboarding

Asking the right questions during interviews can help you identify candidates who align with your organisation's goals and values and have the potential to become high-performing team members. Here are some killer questions you can ask:

1. Growth Mindset:

"Can you share an example of a challenging project you worked on where you had to learn new skills or adapt to a new situation? How did you approach it?"

"Tell me about a time when you faced a setback or failure. How did you handle it, and what did you learn from the experience?"

"What books, courses, or resources have you recently explored to enhance your professional skills?"

2. Purpose Alignment:

"Why are you interested in joining our organisation specifically? What about our mission and values resonates with you?"

"Can you describe a project or initiative you were part of in the past that aligned with your personal values? How did your values contribute to the project's success?"

"What do you see as your long-term contribution to our organisation's mission and goals?"

3. Continuous Learning and Development:

"How do you stay up to date with industry trends and advancements in your field?"

"Can you give an example of a time when you took the initiative to develop a new skill or competency that was not required for your current role?"

"What are your preferred methods for self-assessment and self-improvement in your professional life?"

4. Collaboration and Teamwork:

"Tell me about a project where you had to work closely with a diverse group of individuals. How did you navigate potential differences in opinion or approach?"

"How do you ensure effective communication and collaboration within a team to achieve shared goals?"

"Can you provide an example of a situation where you had to resolve a conflict within a team? How did you handle it, and what was the outcome?"

5. Leadership and Empowerment:

"Have you ever been in a leadership role or acted as a mentor to colleagues? How did you inspire and empower others to excel?"

"How do you balance the need for control with giving team members autonomy and ownership of their work?"

"Can you describe a project where you successfully led a team to achieve exceptional results? What leadership qualities did you demonstrate?"

6. Diversity and Inclusion:

"How do you actively seek out diverse perspectives and voices when working on a project or solving a problem?"

"Tell me about a time when you worked with a team that had members from different cultural backgrounds. How did you ensure everyone's input was valued and included?"

"What actions have you taken to promote diversity and inclusion in your previous workplaces?"

These questions will help you gain valuable insights into a candidate's mindset, values, and experiences, enabling you to make informed decisions about their potential to contribute to your high-performing team.

Leading the Department to Market Success

Marketing has emerged as the compass that guides organisations towards success. It's not merely about selling products; it's about connecting with people, understanding their needs, and crafting compelling stories that resonate. This chapter delves into the realm of marketing mastery, unveiling the keys to leading your department towards unprecedented market success.

The Strategic Imperative

Picture a ship without a captain or a map; it drifts aimlessly, unsure of its destination. Marketing, too, requires strategic guidance to navigate the complex waters of today's marketplace. Your role as a marketing leader is to chart a course, set clear objectives, and steer the ship towards your vision.

Visionary Leadership

In the style of great thought leaders, you must embody visionary leadership. Visionaries see beyond the horizon; they envision possibilities that others may overlook. Your vision is not just about market dominance; it's about creating lasting value for your customers and your organisation.

The Power of Purpose

Purpose is the North Star that guides your marketing efforts. What is your department's purpose? Is it to inspire, educate, entertain, or solve a problem? A clear sense of purpose is the cornerstone of successful marketing. It ignites passion within your team and resonates with your audience.

Understanding Your Audience

Sinek and Robbins may not be directly quoted, but their wisdom echoes in the importance of understanding your audience. Your customers are the heart of your marketing strategy. Dive deep into their desires, pains, and aspirations. Craft you're messaging to speak directly to their hearts.

Content That Connects

Content is the bridge between your brand and your audience. Your content should evoke emotion, inspire action, and leave a lasting impact. Share stories that touch the soul, insights that enlighten, and solutions that empower.

Adaptability and Agility

The marketing landscape is ever-changing, much like the dynamic style of Sinek's talks. To achieve mastery, your department must embrace adaptability and agility. Stay attuned to emerging trends, technologies, and consumer behaviours. Be ready to pivot your strategies when necessary.

Data-Driven Decision Making

Robbins' emphasis on constant improvement finds its place here. Data is the compass that guides your marketing ship. Analyse metrics, customer feedback, and market research to refine your strategies continuously. Don't just rely on gut feelings; let data drive your decisions.

Collaboration and Innovation

Foster collaboration between your marketing team and other departments. Innovative ideas often arise at the intersection of diverse perspectives. Encourage brainstorming sessions, cross-functional projects, and a culture that celebrates creativity.

Leadership's Role in Empowerment

Robbins' teachings on personal empowerment can be applied to leadership within your marketing department. Empower your team to take ownership of their projects, make decisions, and explore new avenues. An empowered team is a motivated and innovative one.

Measuring Success

Marketing mastery is not about guesswork; it's about measurable outcomes. Define clear KPIs (Key Performance Indicators) aligned with your objectives. Regularly assess progress, adjust strategies as needed, and celebrate milestones. Success is not a destination; it's a journey of continuous improvement.

Embracing Challenges

Marketing mastery requires the ability to embrace challenges and setbacks. Every obstacle is an opportunity to learn, adapt, and grow. Use failures as steppingstones to greater success.

Ethical Marketing

In the style of Sinek's emphasis on ethics and values, ensure that your marketing strategies align with ethical standards. Transparency, honesty, and authenticity are the cornerstones of trust-building in today's market. Uphold these principles in all your marketing efforts.

Global Perspective

In a world where boundaries are blurring, a global perspective is essential. Your marketing mastery should extend beyond borders. Understand cultural nuances, preferences, and market dynamics in different regions. Tailor your strategies to resonate with diverse audiences.

The Legacy of Mastery

Marketing mastery is not a static achievement; it's an ongoing journey. As a marketing leader, your role is to inspire your team, foster innovation, and navigate the ever-changing currents of the market. By embracing purpose, data, collaboration, and ethical values, you can steer your department towards unparalleled success. Remember, marketing mastery is not just about selling; it's about creating lasting impressions and building relationships that stand the test of time. As you lead your team with vision, purpose, and unwavering dedication, you will leave a legacy of marketing excellence that resonates in the hearts and minds of your audience.

Strategies for Revenue Growth

Welcome to the exhilarating realm of sales excellence, where every interaction is an opportunity, and revenue growth isn't just a goal – it's a certainty. I'm here to guide you through the high-octane strategies that will transform you into a sales dynamo.

The Pursuit of Mastery

Sales is no place for the timid; it's a battleground where champions emerge. It's a relentless pursuit of excellence, a game where those who embrace challenges with fervour and tenacity come out on top. As you step into this arena, remember that every challenge conceals an opportunity waiting to be seized.

The Force of Mindset

Your mindset is the linchpin of success in sales. How you perceive challenges, setbacks, and rejections will define your journey. In the face of adversity, do you crumble, or do you rise stronger? Embrace each obstacle as a steppingstone toward your goals, and let your mindset propel you forward.

Building Unshakable Relationships

Sales is not solely about transactions; it's about building lasting relationships. Dive deep into your clients' needs, earn their trust, and become their indispensable partner. Your clients should see you as the one who understands, cares, and consistently delivers value.

The Art of the Close

Closing deals is the heartbeat of sales. When you're in the final stretch, your energy should be infectious. Your passion for your product or service should shine through, compelling prospects to act. You are the catalyst that transforms potential into profit.

Value as the North Star

Value isn't a buzzword; it's your guiding star. Your offering should genuinely enhance your clients' lives or businesses. Are you crystal clear on the transformation your product or service brings? If not, go back to the drawing board until you are.

Precision in Prospecting

Time is your most precious asset. Don't squander it on unqualified leads. Just as a sharpshooter doesn't waste bullets, profile your ideal clients and target them with precision. Focus your energy where it counts, on prospects with a higher likelihood to convert.

Mastering Objections

Objections are not roadblocks; they're gateways to persuasion. With each objection, you have an opportunity to demonstrate your expertise and address your client's concerns. Welcome objections as invitations to showcase your mastery.

Relentless Growth

Sales excellence is not static; it's a dynamic journey of continuous growth. Invest in your knowledge, sales techniques, and personal development. The more you learn and grow, the more valuable you become to your clients.

The Fire of Persistence

Persistence is your secret weapon. When faced with rejection and setbacks, your unwavering resolve will set you apart. Be the relentless force that refuses to bow to adversity.

Coaching Questions for Sales Excellence

1. What is your vision for your sales career, and how are you actively pursuing it?
2. How do you maintain a resolute and positive mindset in the face of challenges?
3. Describe a recent successful sale. What strategies did you employ to close it?
4. How do you cultivate and nurture meaningful client relationships?
5. During objections, how do you approach each one to turn them into opportunities?
6. What steps do you take to continuously improve your product knowledge and sales skills?
7. Can you share a situation where your persistence paid off in a challenging sales scenario?
8. Are you confident in articulating the unique value your product or service offers to clients?

9. How do you prioritise your time and focus on high-potential prospects?

10. Explain how you maintain and channel high energy throughout the sales process.

11. How do you cope with rejection, and what strategies do you use to bounce back swiftly?

12. Share a client success story resulting from your sales efforts.

13. What are your sales targets, and what actionable steps are you taking to meet them?

14. How do you keep your schedule organised to ensure no potential leads slip through the cracks?

15. Describe a situation where you had to adapt your sales approach to address a client's unique needs.

16. How do you build and reinforce trust and credibility with your clients?

17. What methods do you use to gauge the effectiveness of your sales strategies and make necessary adjustments?

18. Can you share a challenging sales experience and the strategies you employed to overcome it?

19. What resources or mentors do you rely on for continuous sales training and development?

20. How do you balance work and personal life while pursuing sales excellence?

21. What motivates and fuels your drive for success in your sales career?

22. Share an instance where you successfully upsold a client. What approach did you take?

23. How do you embrace competition in the sales arena, and how do you differentiate yourself?

24. What role does goal setting play in your sales success, and how do you monitor your progress?

25. How do you leverage technology and tools to streamline your sales processes and maximise efficiency?

26. Remember, sales excellence is not an end goal; it's an exhilarating journey of perpetual growth and achievement. Conquer challenges, embrace opportunities, and become the unstoppable force that propels you toward unparalleled success in the world of sales.

I couldn't jump to the next chapter with some of my personal narrative around sales. Warning, I may go on a bit. There are many gurus of old that one could talk about, but I've chose the "Zig", mainly because it's a cool name.

Zig Ziglar was a master of the spoken word, and his journey from humble beginnings to becoming an internationally renowned motivational speaker and sales trainer is a testament to the power of determination and self-improvement. Ziglar's personal transformation was a story of overcoming adversity and embracing the principles he would later espouse.

At the heart of Zig Ziglar's philosophy lay the belief that success in sales and life was not solely about techniques or tactics; it was about the development of the whole person. He emphasised the importance of character, integrity, and ethical conduct as the foundation of long-term success in sales. Ziglar's message was not just about closing deals; it was about building meaningful, enduring relationships with clients.

Ziglar's work was deeply rooted in the power of positive thinking. He often said, "Your attitude, not your aptitude, will determine your altitude." His teachings emphasised the significance of a positive mindset as a catalyst for success. In an industry where rejection is common and resilience is paramount, Ziglar's insights on maintaining a positive attitude in the face of adversity remain invaluable.

Persuasion was a cornerstone of Ziglar's approach to sales. He understood that effective persuasion wasn't about manipulation but about connecting with people on a deeper level. He believed that the most successful salespeople were those who genuinely cared about their customers and sought to solve their problems. Ziglar's lessons on the art of persuasion continue to be relevant in today's customer-centric sales landscape.

The enduring relevance of Zig Ziglar's work can be attributed to several factors. Firstly, his principles are rooted in timeless human values. Concepts like honesty, integrity, and empathy transcend generational shifts and technological advancements. In a world that often seems to change overnight, these core values remain steadfast.

Secondly, Ziglar's teachings were never solely about sales techniques. They were about personal growth and development. He believed that success in sales was a reflection of one's character and mindset. This holistic approach to success ensures that Ziglar's wisdom is applicable not only in sales but in various facets of life.

I LOVE THIS STUFF. Sorry, I couldn't contain myself. Let's carry on.

Zig Ziglar's work embodies the essence of why "the oldies are the goodies" in the world of sales and personal development. His teachings, grounded in timeless principles, have stood the test of time. They offer a compass for navigating the complexities of the modern sales landscape, which may be filled with technological innovations and ever evolving strategies but remains fundamentally driven by human interaction and relationships.

In a world where attention spans are shrinking and quick fixes are sought after, Ziglar's emphasis on long-term, relationship-focused selling reminds us that there are no shortcuts to genuine success. Building trust and rapport with clients takes time, effort, and a commitment to the principles of integrity and empathy. Ziglar's teachings serve as a reminder that meaningful connections and ethical conduct are the bedrock of sustainable success.

Zig Ziglar's work continues to inspire sales professionals today for several reasons. First and foremost, his authenticity and sincerity in delivering his message resonated with audiences then and continue to do so now. His words were not mere platitudes but reflections of his own journey and convictions.

Moreover, Ziglar's work is relatable because it addresses the core challenges and aspirations of sales professionals. He understood the highs and lows of the sales profession—the elation of closing a deal and the frustration of facing rejection. His messages of resilience, perseverance, and maintaining a positive attitude in the face of adversity are evergreen.

Zig Ziglar's enduring impact on the world of sales and personal development is a testament to the enduring power of his message. His work reminds us that the fundamentals of success—integrity, empathy, positivity, and ethical conduct—remain constant in an ever-changing world.

As I delve into Ziglar's work, I'm reminded that the oldies truly are the goodies. His teachings continue to inspire sales professionals not because they are outdated, but because they are timeless. Zig Ziglar's legacy serves as a guiding light for those who seek success built on a foundation of character, integrity, and genuine human connection—a legacy that will continue to inspire generations to come.

Streamlining Departmental Efficiency

Efficiency is the conductor's wand that sets the tempo. It's the fuel that propels departments forward, enabling them to orchestrate their operations with finesse. In this chapter, we'll plunge into the dynamic realm of operations optimisation\, iWe'll explore the art of streamlining departmental efficiency, not just as a process but as a philosophy that drives progress.

The Rhythm of Efficiency

Efficiency isn't a mere buzzword; it's the heartbeat of successful operations. It's about doing more with less, accomplishing tasks swiftly, and eliminating wasteful practices. The pursuit of efficiency is not a one-time endeavour; it's a continuous journey, an ethos that permeates the department.

Purpose-Driven Efficiency

Efficiency should not be pursued for its own sake but in service of a greater purpose. Leaders and team members must understand why efficiency matters, how it contributes to the department's mission, and why it's essential for achieving overarching goals.

Streamlining Processes

A key facet of operations optimisation\ is the streamlining of processes. Departments should critically assess their workflows, identifying bottlenecks, redundancies, and inefficiencies. Streamlining processes not only saves time but also reduces the risk of errors.

Leveraging Technology

In an era of digital transformation, departments must harness the power of technology. Automation, data analytics, and digital tools can significantly enhance efficiency. However, technology should be viewed as an enabler, not a magic bullet. It's essential to choose and implement technology strategically, aligning it with departmental objectives.

The Power of Standardization

Standardization is the cornerstone of efficiency. Departments should establish clear standard operating procedures (SOPs) that define how tasks are to be executed. Standardization promotes consistency, reduces errors, and facilitates training.

Effective Resource Management

Efficiency extends to resource management. Departments should optimise the allocation of resources, including personnel, budget, and time. Effective resource management ensures that no resources are wasted or underutilised.

Continuous Improvement Culture

Efficiency is not a destination; it's a journey. Departments should cultivate a culture of continuous improvement. Team members at all levels should be encouraged to identify opportunities for efficiency gains and suggest improvements.

Data-Driven Decision Making

Data is the compass that guides efficient operations. Departments should rely on data-driven decision-making processes. This involves collecting, analysing, and interpreting data to inform choices, monitor progress, and adjust strategies as needed.

Effective Communication Channels

Inefficient communication can hinder operations. Departments should establish effective communication channels, ensuring that information flows seamlessly and reaches the right recipients in a timely manner. Clear communication reduces misunderstandings and delays.

Role Clarity and Delegation

Efficient operations depend on role clarity. Team members should have a clear understanding of their roles and responsibilities. Leaders should delegate tasks based on team members' strengths and expertise, avoiding micromanagement.

Empowering Teams

Efficiency is not just about top-down optimisation; it's also about empowering teams. Leaders should foster an environment where team members feel comfortable suggesting improvements and taking ownership of their work.

Efficient Supply Chain Management

In departments that rely on supply chains, optimizing the supply chain process is paramount. This involves evaluating suppliers, logistics, inventory management, and distribution channels to reduce costs and improve delivery times.

Cost Control and Budgeting

Efficiency often equates to cost control. Departments should closely monitor expenses, identify cost-saving opportunities, and create budgets that align with departmental objectives. Cost efficiency is a key component of overall efficiency.

Customer-Centric Approach

Efficiency isn't just an internal matter; it extends to external relationships. Departments should adopt a customer-centric approach, focusing on meeting customer needs promptly and effectively. Happy customers are not only loyal but also ambassadors for the department.

Sustainability and Efficiency

Efficiency should not come at the cost of sustainability. Departments should consider the environmental impact of their operations and seek ways to minimise it. Sustainability and efficiency can go hand in hand, creating a win-win scenario.

Resilience and Adaptability

Efficiency should not make departments rigid. It should enhance resilience and adaptability. Efficient operations can pivot quickly in response to unexpected challenges, maintaining stability in turbulent times.

Measuring Efficiency

Efficiency should be quantifiable. Departments should establish key performance indicators (KPIs) to measure efficiency in various areas. Regular assessments help identify areas that need improvement and track progress.

THE TAKEAWAY: Orchestrating Efficiency

Operations optimisation is not just a choice; it's an imperative. Efficiency is the conductor's wand that orchestrates operations with precision and harmony. Effective departments don't just aim for efficiency; they make it a way of life. Efficiency isn't a fleeting tune; it's the rhythm that sustains the department's progress and keeps it in sync with its mission. It's the art of conducting operations with finesse, reducing waste, and ensuring that every action contributes to the department's success. It's about orchestrating efficiency, not as a standalone process, but as the very essence of how the department operates, continuously improving, innovating, and thriving in the ever-changing landscape of business.

Fostering a Culture of Ideas

Innovation is not just a buzzword; it's the lifeline that keeps departments thriving in the face of change. Innovation is the spark that ignites progress, and creativity is the fuel that keeps it burning bright. In this chapter, we'll dive headfirst into the dynamic realm of innovation and creativity, We'll explore how to cultivate a culture of ideas that propels departments to new heights.

The Power of Innovation

Innovation isn't reserved for the R&D department; it's a mindset that should permeate every corner of an organisation. It's about finding new solutions, improving processes, and staying ahead of the curve. Innovation is not a luxury; it's a necessity for staying competitive in today's fast-paced business world.

Creativity as a Catalyst

Creativity is the wellspring from which innovation flows. It's about thinking differently, challenging the status quo, and pushing boundaries. Creativity isn't limited to the arts; it's the essence of problem-solving and ideation. Departments should recognise that everyone has creative potential waiting to be unleashed.

The Innovation Ecosystem

Innovation doesn't happen in isolation. It thrives in an ecosystem that supports and nurtures it. Departments should create an environment where team members are encouraged to explore new ideas, experiment, and take calculated risks. The innovation ecosystem should value diversity of thought and foster collaboration.

Inspiring Curiosity

Curiosity is the cornerstone of creativity. Leaders should inspire curiosity by asking questions, encouraging exploration, and challenging assumptions. Curiosity is the driving force behind the quest for new ideas and solutions.

Failure as a Steppingstone

Innovation often involves trial and error. Departments should view failure not as a setback but as a valuable learning experience. Leaders should create a culture where team members feel safe to take risks, knowing that failure is a steppingstone to success.

Cross-Pollination of Ideas

Innovation flourishes when ideas from different domains intersect. Departments should encourage cross-pollination by bringing together team members with diverse backgrounds and perspectives. Creative collisions can lead to ground-breaking innovations.

Embracing Constraints

Creativity thrives under constraints. Rather than viewing constraints as limitations, departments should see them as opportunities to think creatively. Constraints force team members to find innovative solutions within existing parameters.

Design Thinking

Design thinking is a problem-solving approach that places the user's needs at the centre of the process. It involves empathy, ideation, prototyping, and testing. Departments should incorporate design thinking principles into their innovation efforts.

Continuous Learning and Development

Innovation requires continuous learning. Departments should invest in the development of team members, providing training and resources to enhance their skills and knowledge. Lifelong learning is a cornerstone of a creative and innovative workforce.

Encouraging Intrapreneurship

Intrapreneurs are employees who exhibit an entrepreneurial spirit within the organisation. They identify opportunities, take ownership of projects, and drive innovation. Departments should create avenues for intrapreneurship to flourish.

Measuring and Recognising Innovation

Innovation should be measurable. Departments should establish key performance indicators (KPIs) to track the impact of innovation efforts. Recognising and celebrating innovative achievements motivates team members to continue generating ideas.

Transparency and Collaboration

Innovation is a collaborative effort. Departments should foster transparency and open communication, ensuring that ideas are shared and discussed. Collaboration platforms and brainstorming sessions can be instrumental in idea generation.

Prototyping and Testing

Innovation isn't just about ideation; it's about turning ideas into tangible solutions. Departments should encourage prototyping and testing to validate concepts and gather feedback. Rapid iteration is a hallmark of successful innovation.

Protecting Intellectual Property

Innovation often involves the creation of intellectual property. Departments should have policies and processes in place to protect intellectual property and ensure that innovators are appropriately recognised and rewarded.

Sustainability and Ethical Innovation

Innovation should align with sustainability and ethical principles. Departments should consider the environmental and social impacts of their innovations, seeking to create positive change rather than harm.

Scaling Innovation

Innovation is not limited to small-scale ideas. Departments should have a strategy for scaling successful innovations and integrating them into the broader organisation.

THE TAKEAWAY: Igniting the Creative Fire

Innovation and creativity are not just optional extras; they're the heartbeats that infuse departments with vitality and resilience. The dynamic landscape of business, technology isn't just a tool; it's a catalyst that propels departments into uncharted territory. It's the bridge that connects the present with the future, and digital transformation is the journey across that bridge. In this chapter, we embark on a thought-provoking exploration of technology in business. We'll delve into the profound impact of digital transformation and how it reshapes the very essence of how departments operate and innovate.

Harnessing Digital Transformation

The Digital Revolution

We stand at the precipice of a digital revolution that's rewriting the rules of business. Technology is evolving at an exponential pace, reshaping industries, redefining customer expectations, and challenging established norms. It's not merely a matter of keeping up; it's about embracing the possibilities that technology offers.

From Disruption to Opportunity

Digital transformation isn't just a response to disruption; it's an opportunity for departments to lead the charge. It's a chance to reinvent business models, streamline operations, and create unprecedented value for customers. In this digital age, the only constant is change, and the departments that thrive are those that navigate change with agility.

Data as the New Currency

In the digital realm, data is the new currency. Every interaction, transaction, and engagement generate data. Departments must harness the power of data analytics to gain insights, make informed decisions, and create personalised customer experiences. The ability to transform data into actionable intelligence is a competitive advantage.

Customer-Centric Transformation

Digital transformation places the customer at the heart of operations. It's about understanding customer needs, preferences, and behaviours in real time. Departments should use technology to create seamless, personalised experiences that build customer loyalty and drive growth.

The Ecosystem of Connectivity

Digital transformation doesn't occur in isolation. It's part of a larger ecosystem of connectivity. Departments should leverage technologies like the Internet of Things (IoT), cloud computing, and APIs to create interconnected systems that enhance efficiency and agility.

Embracing Automation and AI

Automation and artificial intelligence (AI) are revolutionising how departments operate. Routine tasks can be automated, freeing up human talent for more strategic endeavours. AI can analyse vast datasets, predict trends, and even provide insights that humans might overlook.

The Challenge of Cybersecurity

As technology advances, so do the threats. Cybersecurity is a critical aspect of digital transformation. Departments must prioritise the protection of sensitive data and build robust cybersecurity measures to safeguard against cyberattacks.

Reskilling and Upskilling

Digital transformation requires a workforce with the skills to harness technology effectively. Departments should invest in reskilling and upskilling team members, ensuring that they have the digital literacy and capabilities needed to thrive in the digital age.

Ethical Considerations

As technology becomes increasingly integrated into business operations, ethical considerations come to the forefront. Departments should navigate digital transformation with a strong ethical compass, considering the impact of their actions on privacy, society, and the environment.

Innovation and Adaptability

Digital transformation is not a one-time event; it's a continuous journey. Departments should foster a culture of innovation and adaptability, encouraging team members to explore emerging technologies and experiment with new ideas.

Regulatory Compliance

The digital landscape is subject to regulatory changes. Departments should stay informed about relevant regulations and ensure that their digital practices comply with legal requirements.

Sustainability in the Digital Age

Digital transformation should align with sustainability goals. Departments should consider the environmental impact of their digital initiatives and seek to reduce their carbon footprint.

The Human Element

Amidst the digital whirlwind, the human element remains indispensable. Technology should augment human capabilities, not replace them. Departments should use technology to empower employees, enabling them to focus on tasks that require creativity, critical thinking, and empathy.

Strategic Partnerships

In the digital era, strategic partnerships are more vital than ever. Collaborations with technology vendors, start-ups, and other organisations can provide access to cutting-edge solutions and expand the department's capabilities.

Measuring Success in the Digital Age

Departments should establish key performance indicators (KPIs) to measure the success of their digital transformation initiatives. These KPIs should align with departmental objectives and reflect the impact of digital transformation on business outcomes.

THE TAKEAWAY: The Digital Frontier

Digital transformation isn't just a technological evolution; it's a profound shift in mindset and approach. It's about embracing the possibilities of technology, reimagining business models, and forging a path into the digital unknown. Departments don't just adapt to technology; they harness it to reshape industries, create exceptional customer experiences, and drive innovation. Digital transformation is not just a choice; it's a mandate for survival and success in a digital-first world. It's about recognising that the future belongs to those who dare to dream, those who see technology not as a challenge but as an opportunity to build a brighter, more connected, and more sustainable future for departments and the world they serve, effective departments don't wait for innovation to happen; they cultivate a culture where it can thrive. Innovation is not a solitary act; it's a collective effort fuelled by curiosity, creativity, and a relentless pursuit of better solutions. It's about igniting the creative fire within every team member, fostering a culture where ideas are cherished, and where innovation isn't just a process but a way of life. It's about realising that the future belongs to those who dare to dream, challenge convention, and transform ideas into reality.

Delivering Exceptional Service

One truth stands tall and unwavering: customers are the lifeblood of any organisation. The success of a department hinges not merely on products or services but on the relationships forged with those it serves. In this chapter, we journey into the heart of customer-centric leadership. We'll explore how passionate customer-centric leadership isn't just a strategy; it's a way of life that transforms departments into beacons of exceptional service.

The Customer-Centric Revolution

The customer-centric revolution is not a fad; it's a seismic shift that's redefining how departments operate. It's the recognition that customers are more than transactions; they are partners in success. Customer-centric leadership is not about bending to every customer whim but about understanding their needs, aspirations, and challenges.

Leading with Empathy

Customer-centric leadership begins with empathy. It's about stepping into the customer's shoes, seeing the world from their perspective, and truly understanding their pain points and desires. It's the foundation upon which exceptional service is built.

Passion for Service Excellence

Passionate customer-centric leaders don't settle for mediocrity; they crave service excellence. They see every interaction as an opportunity to exceed expectations, to create memorable moments that leave a lasting impression. Excellence isn't a goal; it's a standard.

Building Customer Relationships

In a transactional world, customer-centric leaders focus on building relationships. They seek to forge connections that go beyond a single purchase. They know that loyal customers are not just repeat buyers; they are advocates who sing the department's praises.

The Art of Active Listening

Customer-centric leaders are exceptional listeners. They don't merely hear words; they listen to understand. They ask probing questions, dig deep into customer feedback, and use it to drive continuous improvement.

Personalisation as a Cornerstone

Customers are not one-size-fits-all, and neither should be the service they receive. Customer-centric leaders embrace personalisation, tailoring their approach to meet individual needs and preferences.

Empowerment of Team Members

Exceptional service doesn't happen in a vacuum. Customer-centric leaders empower their team members, giving them the autonomy to make decisions that benefit the customer. They trust their team's judgment and support their growth.

Consistency Across Channels

In an omnichannel world, consistency is key. Customer-centric leaders ensure that the customer experience remains seamless whether customers interact with the department online, in-store, or through other channels.

Anticipating Customer Needs

Predicting customer needs is the mark of a true customer-centric leader. They don't wait for customers to ask; they proactively offer solutions and suggestions based on their deep understanding of the customer's goals.

Transparency and Trust

Trust is the bedrock of customer relationships. Customer-centric leaders are transparent in their interactions, setting clear expectations and delivering on promises. They build trust through honesty and reliability.

Handling Complaints with Grace

No department is immune to complaints. Customer-centric leaders view complaints not as problems but as opportunities to showcase their commitment to service excellence. They handle complaints with grace, addressing issues promptly and finding solutions that leave customers delighted.

Measuring Customer Satisfaction

Customer-centric leaders don't rely on gut feelings; they measure customer satisfaction. They establish key performance indicators (KPIs) and collect customer feedback to assess the impact of their service initiatives.

Continuous Improvement

The pursuit of service excellence is never-ending. Customer-centric leaders foster a culture of continuous improvement, always seeking ways to enhance the customer experience and stay ahead of changing customer expectations.

Cultivating a Customer-Centric Culture

Exceptional service is not the responsibility of a single department or team; it's a cultural mindset. Customer-centric leaders cultivate a culture where every team member, from the front lines to the back office, understands their role in delivering exceptional service.

Empathy in Crisis

In challenging times, empathy shines even brighter. Customer-centric leaders navigate crises with grace and compassion, putting the well-being of their customers at the forefront.

Celebrating Customer Success Stories

Customer-centric leaders celebrate customer success stories. They recognise and share stories of exceptional service, inspiring their team members to strive for greatness.

Passion and Persistence

Customer-centric leadership is not for the faint of heart. It requires passion, persistence, and an unwavering commitment to excellence. It's a journey of continuous growth and learning.

THE TAKEAWAY: The Heartbeat of Exceptional Service

Customer-centric leadership isn't just a strategy; it's a way of life. It's about recognising that departments don't exist in isolation; they exist to serve customers and enrich their lives. Departments don't merely satisfy customers; they create raving fans who champion their cause. Customer-centric leadership is not a destination; it's a journey of unwavering commitment to service excellence, a journey that transforms departments into beacons of exceptional service and leaves a legacy of customer delight that transcends transactions and endures through time. It's about understanding that exceptional service isn't just a business strategy; it's a profound expression of care, a way of saying, "We see you, we value you, and we are here to serve you with excellence."

I'm going to add something further to the takeaway. Welcome to the world of Disney.

Walt Disney, the visionary behind the beloved Disney brand, is synonymous with creativity, storytelling, and the magic of imagination. Beyond the enchanting tales and iconic characters, Walt Disney had an extraordinary impact on the world of customer service. His commitment to delivering exceptional experiences has left an indelible mark, making Disney not just an entertainment giant but also a customer service trailblazer.

Walt Disney's journey into customer service excellence began with a dream—a dream to create a place where families could escape the ordinary and immerse themselves in a world of enchantment. This vision culminated in the opening of Disneyland in 1955, the first-ever theme park of its kind.

Disneyland was more than an amusement park; it was a place where customer service was elevated to an art form. Walt Disney understood that to create a truly magical experience, every aspect of customer service had to be considered, from the moment guests entered the park to the moment they left.

One of Walt Disney's remarkable contributions to customer service was his unwavering commitment to detail. He believed that every detail, no matter how small, contributed to the overall guest experience. From meticulously designed attractions to well-maintained gardens and friendly staff, Disney parks were a testament to the power of attention to detail.

Disney's obsession with detail extended to the cleanliness of the parks, the presentation of food, and even the behaviour of cast members (as Disney employees are known). This attention to detail created an environment where guests felt valued and cared for, setting a standard for customer service excellence.

Walt Disney understood that customer service was not merely about transactions; it was about creating lasting memories. He believed that a visit to Disneyland should be an unforgettable experience that guests would cherish for a lifetime. This philosophy permeated every aspect of Disney parks.

From characters roaming the park to interact with children, to the "Imagineers" who designed immersive attractions, Disney sought to engage all the senses and emotions of visitors. The result was an emotional connection between the brand and its guests—a bond forged through memorable experiences and exceptional customer service.

Disneyland was one of the first places to introduce the concept of "plussing," a term coined by Walt Disney himself. Plussing meant going above and beyond what was expected to surprise and delight customers. This innovative approach to customer service meant constantly improving and innovating, even when things were already excellent.

For example, when a child once asked Walt Disney why he couldn't see the characters backstage, Disney arranged for characters to appear in a grand parade, ensuring that every guest could catch a glimpse of their favourite characters. This commitment to going the extra mile became a hallmark of Disney's approach to customer service.

Walt Disney believed that happy employees would lead to happy customers. He invested in extensive training programs for Disney cast members to ensure they understood the importance of their role in creating magical experiences. He encouraged employees to see themselves as part of the show, not just as service providers.

Disney also empowered employees to make decisions to enhance the guest experience. This autonomy allowed employees to address guest needs promptly, creating a culture of responsiveness and customer-centricity.

Walt Disney's influence on customer service extended far beyond the walls of Disneyland. His principles of attention to detail, creating memories, going above and beyond, and empowering employees have been adopted and adapted by businesses worldwide.

Today, Disney's customer service legacy lives on in Disney theme parks, resorts, and various enterprises. It has also inspired countless other organizations to prioritize customer service excellence as a strategic imperative. The "Disney Way" of delivering exceptional customer experiences continues to be studied and emulated by companies seeking to create magic in their customer interactions.

In conclusion, Walt Disney's genius lay not only in storytelling but also in his profound understanding of customer service. He transformed the ordinary into the extraordinary, ensuring that every visitor to Disneyland felt like a cherished guest. His commitment to attention to detail, creating lasting memories, going above and beyond, and empowering employees set a timeless standard for customer service excellence.

The legacy of Walt Disney lives on not only in the enchanting tales and beloved characters but also in the enduring commitment to making every customer feel special, valued, and part of a magical experience. Walt Disney was not just an entertainment visionary; he was also a pioneer in the art of customer service, and his legacy continues to inspire and shape the world of customer service today.

No Disney characters were harmed in the writing of this book.

CRISIS MANAGEMENT

Leading in Challenging Times

In the ever-changing landscape of business, crises are not a matter of if, but when. Whether it's a global pandemic, economic downturn, natural disaster, or unexpected internal challenges, the ability to navigate crises effectively is a defining characteristic of successful leadership. In this chapter, we delve into the world of crisis management, We'll explore the strategies and principles that guide leaders in turbulent times and conclude with a 10-point plan for managing well in a crisis.

The Unpredictable Nature of Crises

Crises are the uninvited guests that disrupt the status quo. They strike without warning, demanding rapid responses and decisive actions. Effective crisis management is not about preventing crises, as some are beyond control, but about how leaders respond when they occur.

Leadership Amidst Chaos

Leading in a crisis is not for the faint-hearted. It requires a steady hand, a clear mind, and the ability to inspire confidence even in the face of uncertainty. Crisis leadership isn't about avoiding fear and anxiety; it's about managing them effectively.

The Crucial Role of Communication

Effective crisis communication is the linchpin of crisis management. Leaders must communicate transparently, providing accurate information, setting expectations, and demonstrating empathy. Open lines of communication build trust and calm fears.

Adaptability and Resilience

Crises test the adaptability and resilience of departments and their leaders. Leaders must be willing to pivot, adjust strategies, and make tough decisions. Resilience involves not just surviving the storm but emerging stronger on the other side.

Collaboration and Teamwork

Crises often require a collective effort. Leaders must foster collaboration among team members, departments, and external partners. A unified approach is more effective than isolated actions.

Resource Allocation and Prioritization

Resource management becomes critical in a crisis. Leaders must allocate resources judiciously, prioritizing initiatives that directly address the crisis. This may involve repurposing budgets, reallocating staff, or seeking additional support.

Scenario Planning and Preparedness

While no one can predict the exact nature of a crisis, leaders can engage in scenario planning and preparedness exercises. These simulations help departments, and their leaders understand potential risks and develop response strategies.

Empathy and Compassion

In times of crisis, empathy and compassion are invaluable. Leaders should recognise the emotional toll on team members and offer support. A compassionate approach fosters resilience and builds team cohesion.

Measuring Impact and Adjusting Strategies

Crisis management is not a one-time event; it's an ongoing process. Leaders must continually assess the impact of their actions and adjust strategies as needed. Flexibility is key to effective crisis management.

The 10-Point Plan for Managing Well in a Crisis

Preparation is Key: Develop a robust crisis management plan well in advance. Identify potential risks, establish response protocols, and train your team on crisis procedures.

Stay Informed: Maintain a deep understanding of the evolving situation. Continuously gather information from reliable sources to make informed decisions.

Transparent Communication: Communicate early, often, and transparently with all stakeholders. Share accurate information, address concerns, and provide guidance.

Empower Your Team: Delegate responsibilities and empower your team members to make decisions within their areas of expertise. Trust your team's judgment.

Prioritise Safety: The safety and well-being of your team and stakeholders should be the top priority. Implement safety measures and provide support where needed.

Resource Allocation: Allocate resources wisely, focusing on critical areas that address the crisis. Be prepared to reallocate resources as the situation evolves.

Adapt and Innovate: Be open to innovative solutions and adapt to changing circumstances. Flexibility is essential in crisis management.

Lead by Example: Demonstrate composure, empathy, and resilience. Your team will look to you for guidance and inspiration.

Feedback and Evaluation: Establish mechanisms for feedback and continuous evaluation of crisis response efforts. Learn from the crisis to enhance future preparedness.

Recovery and Learning: After the crisis subsides, lead the department in a process of recovery and learning. Analyse what went well and what could be improved for future crises.

THE TAKEAWAY: The Crucible of Leadership

Crisis management isn't just a skill; it's a crucible that forges leaders of unwavering strength and resilience. It's a test of character, a proving ground where leaders rise to the occasion, guiding their departments through the storm with fortitude and grace. Crisis management isn't about avoiding adversity; it's about navigating it with wisdom and resolve. It's about understanding that while crises may be inevitable, the way we respond to them defines our legacy as leaders. It's about recognising that in the darkest of times, true leaders emerge, guiding their departments not just to survive but to thrive in the face of adversity.

....

Charting a Course for Departmental Success

The journey towards success isn't a random walk; it's a deliberate and calculated path. It's about strategic planning—a methodical approach to steering the department toward its objectives. In this chapter, we explore the principles of strategic planning that have resonated through the ages, echoing the wisdom of those who mastered the art of purposeful direction without explicitly mentioning them.

The Essence of Strategic Planning

Strategic planning is the compass that guides departments through the uncharted waters of business. It's the process of setting goals, making informed decisions, and allocating resources to achieve long-term success. Like ancient navigators charting their course by the stars, strategic planners use data and insight to navigate the complexities of the business landscape.

Clarity of Purpose

At the heart of strategic planning is clarity of purpose. Leaders must articulate a clear and compelling vision for the department. This vision serves as the North Star, guiding all actions and decisions towards a common destination.

Understanding the Terrain

Just as a navigator studies the maps and charts of the sea, strategic planners must understand the terrain of their industry. They analyse market trends, competitive landscapes, and emerging opportunities to make informed decisions.

The Power of Focus

Strategic planning demands focus. It requires prioritizing objectives and resources to maximise impact. A scattergun approach dissipates energy and dilutes results. A focused strategy hones the department's efforts like a finely crafted blade.

Risk Assessment

Like ancient explorers weighing the perils of uncharted waters, strategic planners assess risks. They identify potential obstacles and develop contingency plans. Risk mitigation is a critical aspect of strategic planning.

Resource Allocation

Strategic planning involves allocating resources strategically. This includes budgets, personnel, and time. Planners ensure that resources are directed towards activities that align with the department's goals.

Agility and Adaptability

Even the best-planned journeys encounter unexpected storms. Strategic planners must embrace agility and adaptability. They remain open to course corrections, adjusting strategies as circumstances evolve.

Measuring Progress

A strategic plan without measurement is like a ship without a compass. Planners establish key performance indicators (KPIs) to track progress. Regular assessments help determine whether the department is on course or needs adjustment.

Long-Term Vision

Strategic planning is not a short-term endeavour. It's about thinking beyond immediate concerns and considering the long-term implications of decisions. A department's success is measured not just by today's results but by its enduring impact.

Collaborative Decision-Making

Strategic planners often involve team members in the decision-making process. Collaborative decision-making harnesses the diverse perspectives and expertise within the department.

Resilience in the Face of Setbacks

Just as ancient explorers faced setbacks and trials, departments will encounter challenges on their strategic journeys. Resilience is the ability to weather these setbacks and press onward with determination.

Communication and Alignment

A strategic plan is effective only when everyone in the department understands and aligns with it. Leaders must communicate the plan clearly and consistently to ensure that all team members are rowing in the same direction.

Ethical Considerations

The stoic principles of virtue and integrity resonate through strategic planning. Ethical considerations are paramount in decision-making. Planners must uphold the department's values and act with integrity.

Sustainability and Responsibility

Strategic planning should consider the department's impact on the environment in the vibrant tapestry of business, silos are the enemy of progress. Departments that operate in isolation, like isolated islands, often miss out on the wealth of opportunities that cross-functional collaboration can unlock. In this punchy chapter, we'll dive into the dynamic world of cross-functional collaboration and explore how building bridges between departments can supercharge innovation, efficiency, and success.

The Power of Synergy

Cross-functional collaboration isn't just a feel-good concept; it's a strategic powerhouse. It's about harnessing the combined expertise and perspectives of various departments to tackle complex challenges and seize opportunities that no single department can address alone.

Breaking Down Silos

Silos are the invisible barriers that hinder communication and cooperation between departments. Punchy leaders recognise that tearing down these silos is the first step towards creating a culture of collaboration.

Shared Goals and Objectives

Cross-functional collaboration thrives when departments share common goals and objectives. Punchy leaders align their teams around a shared vision, ensuring that every department understands its role in achieving success.

Open Communication Channels

Effective collaboration requires open and transparent communication channels. Punchy leaders create an environment where team members feel comfortable sharing ideas, feedback, and insights across departmental boundaries.

The Role of Leadership

Leaders play a pivotal role in fostering cross-functional collaboration. Punchy leaders lead by example, actively participating in cross-departmental initiatives and emphasizing the importance of collaboration in their communication.

Cross-Functional Teams

Forming cross-functional teams is a punchy way to drive collaboration. These teams bring together members from different departments to work on specific projects or initiatives, leveraging their diverse expertise.

Diversity of Thought

Cross-functional collaboration is a goldmine of diversity of thought. It brings together individuals with unique perspectives, backgrounds, and skills. Punchy leaders value this diversity and harness it to drive innovation.

Problem-Solving Power

When departments collaborate, they bring a collective problem-solving power to the table. Challenges that may seem insurmountable in isolation become manageable when tackled by a united front of cross-functional teams.

Efficiency and Speed

Cross-functional collaboration streamlines processes and eliminates redundant efforts. Punchy leaders recognise that by working together, departments can achieve tasks more efficiently and with greater speed.

Data-Driven Decisions

Collaboration often involves sharing data and insights. This data-driven approach enables departments to make informed decisions and measure the impact of their collaborative efforts.

Conflict Resolution

Inevitably, conflicts may arise during cross-functional collaboration. Punchy leaders address conflicts head-on, facilitating constructive discussions and finding solutions that benefit the entire department.

Celebrating Wins

Celebrating collaborative successes is a punchy way to reinforce the importance of cross-functional collaboration. Punchy leaders recognise and publicly acknowledge the achievements of cross-functional teams.

Continuous Improvement

Cross-functional collaboration is not a one-time effort; it's an ongoing practice. Punchy leaders seek feedback and continuously refine their collaborative processes to enhance efficiency and effectiveness.

Investing in Technology

Technology can be a powerful enabler of cross-functional collaboration. Departments should invest in collaboration tools and platforms that facilitate communication and information sharing.

Building Trust

Trust is the glue that holds cross-functional collaboration together. Punchy leaders foster trust by consistently delivering on commitments and promoting a culture of integrity.

Cultivating Cross-Functional Leaders

Effective cross-functional leaders are instrumental in driving collaboration. Punchy departments identify and cultivate individuals who excel at bridging departmental divides and inspiring collaboration.

THE TAKEAWAY: The Punchy Nexus of Success

Cross-functional collaboration isn't just a buzzword; it's the secret sauce that turbocharges departments to new heights. It's about recognising that the collective intelligence and capabilities of a united department are far greater than the sum of its parts. Effective departments don't settle for the confines of their own domains; they build bridges across departments, harnessing the power of synergy, diversity, and shared purpose. Collaboration isn't just a choice; it's the punchy nexus of success in a world were interconnectedness and innovation reign supreme. It's about recognising that the future belongs to those who dare to break down the silos, build bridges of collaboration, and forge a path towards excellence that transcends departmental boundaries. And society. Sustainability and social responsibility are increasingly integral to long-term success.

The Legacy of Purposeful Navigation

Strategic planning is not just a tool; it's a legacy of purposeful navigation. It's the understanding that success is not an accident but the result of deliberate choices and actions. Departments don't wander aimlessly; they chart a course that aligns with their purpose and values. Strategic planning is the art of conscious decision-making, where leaders steer their departments toward a future that embodies their vision. It's about recognising that the journey itself is as meaningful as the destination, and that the principles of strategic planning transcend time and circumstance. It's about embracing the wisdom that, while the winds of change may blow, the direction remains true when guided by a strategic plan.

....

Building Bridges Across Departments

Silos are the enemy of progress. Departments that operate in isolation, like isolated islands, often miss out on the wealth of opportunities that cross-functional collaboration can unlock. In this chapter, we'll dive into the dynamic world of cross-functional collaboration and explore how building bridges between departments can supercharge innovation, efficiency, and success.

The Power of Synergy

Cross-functional collaboration isn't just a feel-good concept; it's a strategic powerhouse. It's about harnessing the combined expertise and perspectives of various departments to tackle complex challenges and seize opportunities that no single department can address alone.

Breaking Down Silos

Silos are the invisible barriers that hinder communication and cooperation between departments. Punchy leaders recognise that tearing down these silos is the first step towards creating a culture of collaboration.

Shared Goals and Objectives

Cross-functional collaboration thrives when departments share common goals and objectives. Punchy leaders align their teams around a shared vision, ensuring that every department understands its role in achieving success.

Open Communication Channels

Effective collaboration requires open and transparent communication channels. Punchy leaders create an environment where team members feel comfortable sharing ideas, feedback, and insights across departmental boundaries.

The Role of Leadership

Leaders play a pivotal role in fostering cross-functional collaboration. Punchy leaders lead by example, actively participating in cross-departmental initiatives and emphasizing the importance of collaboration in their communication.

Cross-Functional Teams

Forming cross-functional teams is a punchy way to drive collaboration. These teams bring together members from different departments to work on specific projects or initiatives, leveraging their diverse expertise.

Diversity of Thought

Cross-functional collaboration is a goldmine of diversity of thought. It brings together individuals with unique perspectives, backgrounds, and skills. Punchy leaders value this diversity and harness it to drive innovation.

Problem-Solving Power

When departments collaborate, they bring a collective problem-solving power to the table. Challenges that may seem insurmountable in isolation become manageable when tackled by a united front of cross-functional teams.

Efficiency and Speed

Cross-functional collaboration streamlines processes and eliminates redundant efforts. Punchy leaders recognise that by working together, departments can achieve tasks more efficiently and with greater speed.

Data-Driven Decisions

Collaboration often involves sharing data and insights. This data-driven approach enables departments to make informed decisions and measure the impact of their collaborative efforts.

Conflict Resolution

Inevitably, conflicts may arise during cross-functional collaboration. Punchy leaders address conflicts head-on, facilitating constructive discussions and finding solutions that benefit the entire department.

Celebrating Wins

Celebrating collaborative successes is a punchy way to reinforce the importance of cross-functional collaboration. Punchy leaders recognise and publicly acknowledge the achievements of cross-functional teams.

Continuous Improvement

Cross-functional collaboration is not a one-time effort; it's an ongoing practice. Punchy leaders seek feedback and continuously refine their collaborative processes to enhance efficiency and effectiveness.

Investing in Technology

Technology can be a powerful enabler of cross-functional collaboration. Departments should invest in collaboration tools and platforms that facilitate communication and information sharing.

Building Trust

Trust is the glue that holds cross-functional collaboration together. Punchy leaders foster trust by consistently delivering on commitments and promoting a culture of integrity.

Cultivating Cross-Functional Leaders

Effective cross-functional leaders are instrumental in driving collaboration. Punchy departments identify and cultivate individuals who excel at bridging departmental divides and inspiring collaboration.

THE TAKEAWAY: The Punchy Nexus of Success

Cross-functional collaboration isn't just a buzzword; it's the secret sauce that turbocharges departments to new heights. It's about recognising that the collective intelligence and capabilities of a united department are far greater than the sum of its parts. Effective departments don't settle for the confines of their own domains; they build bridges across departments, harnessing the power of synergy, diversity, and shared purpose. Collaboration isn't just a choice; it's the punchy nexus of success in a world were interconnectedness and innovation reign supreme. It's about recognising that the future belongs to those who dare to break down the silos, build bridges of collaboration, and forge a path towards excellence that transcends departmental boundaries.

Measuring What Matters

The ability to measure and track performance is a cornerstone of success. Departments that rely on a clear set of performance metrics and key performance indicators (KPIs) are better equipped to make informed decisions, set strategic goals, and drive continuous improvement. In this chapter, we will explore the significance of performance metrics and KPIs in modern business and how they are essential tools for measuring what truly matters.

The Power of Measurement

Measurement is the compass that guides departments on their journey towards success. It provides valuable insights into the effectiveness of strategies, the efficiency of operations, and the achievement of objectives. In the fast-paced world of business, measurement is not just a luxury; it's a necessity.

The Purpose of Performance Metrics

Performance metrics are the yardsticks by which departments assess their progress. They provide a clear picture of how well the department is performing against predefined goals and objectives. Metrics serve as a foundation for data-driven decision-making.

The Significance of KPIs

Key Performance Indicators, or KPIs, are a subset of performance metrics that are deemed critical to the department's success. KPIs are specific, measurable, and directly tied to strategic goals. They serve as a focused lens through which leaders can gauge performance.

Aligning Metrics with Strategy

Effective departments align their performance metrics and KPIs with their overall strategic objectives. The metrics chosen should reflect the department's mission and long-term vision, ensuring that every effort contributes to the bigger picture.

Choosing the Right Metrics

Selecting the right performance metrics can be a delicate task. Punchy leaders understand the importance of choosing metrics that are relevant, actionable, and indicative of progress. A metric that doesn't drive meaningful action is of little value.

Quantitative and Qualitative Metrics

Performance metrics encompass both quantitative data, such as revenue, sales numbers, and customer acquisition rates, and qualitative data, such as customer satisfaction scores, employee morale, and brand perception. A well-rounded set of metrics offers a comprehensive view of departmental performance.

Measuring Customer-Centric Success

In today's customer-centric business landscape, departments must pay special attention to metrics related to customer satisfaction, loyalty, and engagement. Customer-centric KPIs can include Net Promoter Score (NPS), Customer Satisfaction (CSAT), and Customer Lifetime Value (CLV).

Operational Efficiency Metrics

To enhance operational efficiency, departments often measure metrics like cycle time, lead time, and resource utilization. These metrics identify bottlenecks, inefficiencies, and areas for improvement in processes.

Financial Metrics

Financial metrics, such as Return on Investment (ROI), Gross Margin, and Cost per Acquisition (CPA), are crucial for assessing the department's financial health and profitability.

Employee Performance Metrics

Measuring employee performance is essential for talent management and retention. Metrics like employee satisfaction, turnover rate, and productivity help leaders identify areas for improvement in workforce management.

The Role of Benchmarking

Benchmarking involves comparing departmental metrics and KPIs to industry standards or competitors' performance. Benchmarking provides context and helps departments set realistic targets for improvement.

Continuous Improvement Through Data Analysis

Effective departments don't stop at measuring performance; they use data analysis to drive continuous improvement. Data-driven insights inform strategic adjustments, process enhancements, and resource reallocation.

The Balanced Scorecard Approach

The Balanced Scorecard is a strategic framework that combines financial, customer, internal process, and learning and growth perspectives. It offers a holistic view of departmental performance, ensuring that progress is not one-sided but well-rounded.

The Challenge of Data Quality

Data quality is paramount in performance measurement. Inaccurate or incomplete data can lead to faulty conclusions and misguided decisions. Punchy departments invest in data quality assurance to ensure the integrity of their metrics.

Effective Data Visualisation

Data visualisation techniques, such as charts, graphs, and dashboards, make complex metrics more accessible and understandable. Effective data presentation aids in communicating performance insights to stakeholders.

Transparent Reporting

Transparency in reporting is essential for building trust among stakeholders. Departments should share performance metrics and KPIs with employees, investors, and customers, demonstrating accountability.

THE TAKEAWAY: Measuring for Success

Performance metrics and KPIs are not just numbers on a spreadsheet; they are the compass that guides departments toward their goals. It's about recognising that data-driven decision-making isn't a luxury; it's a necessity in a world where every action should contribute to the department's success. Successful departments don't leave success to chance; they measure what matters and use the insights to steer their course. Measurement is not just a means to an end; it's the pulse of progress, the heartbeat of improvement, and the roadmap to success. It's about understanding that in a world of constant change, the ability to measure and adapt is the key to not just surviving but thriving.

Navigating Challenges

Conflicts and difficult conversations are not aberrations; they are the crucibles in which strong departments are forged. The ability to navigate these challenges effectively is a hallmark of successful leadership. In this chapter, we will explore the art of conflict resolution and the nuances of difficult conversations—essential skills for building resilient, harmonious, and high-performing departments.

The Inevitability of Conflict

Conflict is an inherent part of human interaction, and departments are no exception. Whether it's differences in opinions, competing priorities, or misunderstandings, conflicts can arise at any time. The key is not to avoid conflicts but to address them constructively.

The Impact of Unresolved Conflict

Unresolved conflicts can fester and escalate, leading to strained relationships, decreased morale, and reduced productivity. Effective conflict resolution is not merely about "putting out fires" but about fostering a culture of open communication and collaboration.

Understanding Conflict Styles

People have different approaches to conflict. Some are confrontational, while others avoid it. Some seek compromise, while others assert their position. Effective leaders understand their own conflict style and adapt it to the situation and the individuals involved.

Active Listening

Active listening is a cornerstone of conflict resolution. It involves not just hearing the words but truly understanding the underlying emotions and concerns. Leaders who actively listen create an environment where others feel heard and valued.

Empathy and Perspective-Taking

Empathy is the ability to put oneself in another's shoes and understand their point of view. Leaders who practice empathy can de-escalate conflicts by showing that they genuinely care about the well-being and perspectives of others.

Choosing the Right Time and Place

Timing matters in conflict resolution. Leaders should choose an appropriate time and private setting for difficult conversations to minimise distractions and create a safe space for dialogue.

The Role of Mediation

In some cases, conflicts may require a neutral third party to mediate. Mediators can help facilitate communication, clarify misunderstandings, and guide both parties toward a resolution.

The Power of Constructive Feedback

Constructive feedback is essential in addressing conflicts and facilitating growth. Leaders should provide feedback that is specific, actionable, and focused on behaviours rather than personal attributes.

Setting Clear Expectations

Preventing conflicts often begins with setting clear expectations and boundaries. Leaders should communicate departmental values, norms, and behavioural expectations to prevent misunderstandings.

Conflict Resolution Models

Several conflict resolution models exist, such as the Thomas-Kilmann Conflict Mode Instrument (TKI) and the Conflict Resolution Styles Model. These models provide frameworks for understanding and addressing conflicts effectively.

Difficult Conversations

Difficult conversations are those that involve sensitive topics, emotions, or high stakes. They can range from performance evaluations and disciplinary actions to salary negotiations and interpersonal conflicts.

Preparing for Difficult Conversations

Effective leaders prepare for difficult conversations by outlining their goals, anticipating potential reactions, and considering various communication strategies. Preparation helps keep the conversation on track.

The Art of Delivering Feedback

Feedback in difficult conversations should be delivered thoughtfully and constructively. Leaders should use "I" statements to express their observations and feelings, avoiding accusatory language.

Managing Emotions

Difficult conversations can be emotionally charged. Leaders must manage their own emotions and help others manage theirs. Deep breathing, active listening, and empathy can all contribute to emotional regulation.

Seeking Win-Win Solutions

In many difficult conversations, leaders should aim for win-win solutions that benefit both parties. This can involve brainstorming alternative solutions, considering compromises, and finding common ground.

The Aftermath: Follow-Up and Resolution

Effective leaders don't end difficult conversations without a plan for follow-up and resolution. They ensure that both parties are committed to any agreed-upon actions and monitor progress.

Fostering a Culture of Respect and Openness

Ultimately, conflict resolution and difficult conversations are not just individual skills; they are indicative of a department's culture. Leaders who model respect, openness, and constructive communication set the tone for the entire department.

THE TAKEAWAY: The Crucible of Leadership

Conflict resolution and difficult conversations are not signs of weakness; they are the crucible in which resilient and high-performing departments are forged. It's about recognising that conflicts, when handled constructively, are opportunities for growth and understanding. Effective leaders don't shy away from difficult conversations; they embrace them to foster respect, collaboration, and mutual understanding. Conflict resolution is not just a skill; it's a testament to the department's commitment to its people and its dedication to creating an environment where differences are addressed with empathy, respect, and a shared commitment to finding common ground. It's about understanding that the path to success isn't always smooth, but it's in navigating the bumps and turns that departments emerge stronger, more cohesive, and better equipped to face the challenges of the future.

....

Investing in Your Team's Growth

One enduring truth remains: the strength of a department lies in its people. Effective leadership is not just about guiding the ship; it's about nurturing the crew to reach their full potential. In this chapter, we will explore the significance of leadership development and how investing in your team's growth is the cornerstone of building resilient, high-performing departments.

The Role of Leadership Development

Leadership development is not an optional add-on; it's the lifeblood of a thriving department. It encompasses a range of activities and strategies designed to enhance the skills, knowledge, and capabilities of leaders at all levels.

Unlocking Potential

Effective leadership development unlocks the potential within individuals, enabling them to take on greater responsibilities and contribute more effectively to the department's success. It's about recognising that every team member has untapped talents and capabilities waiting to be cultivated.

The Mindset of Growth

Leadership development begins with a growth mindset—an attitude that embraces challenges, sees failures as learning opportunities, and believes in the power of continuous improvement. Leaders with a growth mindset inspire their teams to strive for excellence.

Identifying Future Leaders

Leadership development is not just for current leaders; it's also about identifying and nurturing future leaders. Effective departments have a pipeline of talent ready to step into leadership roles when needed.

Mentoring and Coaching

Mentoring and coaching are powerful tools in leadership development. Experienced leaders provide guidance, share their knowledge, and offer support to less experienced team members. Mentoring and coaching relationships foster growth and skills transfer.

Formal Training Programs

Formal training programs, workshops, and seminars provide structured learning opportunities. These programs can cover a wide range of topics, from leadership and communication skills to industry-specific knowledge.

360-Degree Feedback

360-degree feedback involves gathering input on a leader's performance from peers, subordinates, and superiors. This multi-perspective approach helps leaders gain a holistic view of their strengths and areas for improvement.

Leadership Assessments

Assessments, such as personality assessments and leadership competency assessments, provide valuable insights into a leader's strengths and areas for development. These assessments inform personalised development plans.

On-the-Job Learning

Much of leadership development happens on the job. Leaders learn by facing challenges, making decisions, and adapting to new situations. Effective departments provide opportunities for leaders to take on stretch assignments and learn through experience.

Self-Directed Learning

Leaders who take ownership of their development engage in self-directed learning. This involves seeking out resources, books, articles, and online courses to enhance their knowledge and skills.

Cultivating Emotional Intelligence

Emotional intelligence (EQ) is a critical aspect of leadership. Leaders with high EQ understand their emotions and those of others, enabling them to navigate complex interpersonal dynamics and build strong relationships.

Diversity and Inclusion Training

In today's diverse workplace, leaders benefit from diversity and inclusion training. This training helps leaders create inclusive environments where every team member feels valued and heard.

Adaptability and Resilience

Leadership development should include training in adaptability and resilience. These skills enable leaders to thrive in times of change and adversity, guiding their teams through challenges.

The Role of Feedback

Effective leadership development incorporates regular feedback. Leaders should receive constructive feedback on their performance and have opportunities to reflect on their growth journey.

Leadership Development as a Culture

Leadership development is not a one-off event; it's a culture. Effective departments embed leadership development into their DNA, creating a culture that values growth and invests in the development of all team members.

Recognition and Rewards

Leadership development should be recognised and rewarded. Effective departments acknowledge the efforts of leaders who invest in their development and create pathways for career advancement.

THE TAKEAWAY: The Growth-Oriented Department

Leadership development isn't just a luxury; it's a strategic imperative. It's about recognising that the most asset of a department is its people and that investing in their growth is an investment in the department's future. Leaders don't just lead; they empower, inspire, and enable others to rise. Leadership development isn't just a program; it's a commitment to creating a culture of continuous learning, growth, and excellence. It's about understanding that the success of a department is not measured solely by its current achievements but by its capacity to adapt, innovate, and thrive in a future full of challenges and opportunities. It's about recognising that leadership is not a title; it's a journey of self-discovery and growth, where leaders and their teams rise together to reach new heights of success.

Trends and Insights

As technology continues to reshape industries, digital leadership is becoming increasingly vital. Digital leaders understand emerging technologies, data analytics, and the opportunities presented by the digital ecosystem. They leverage technology to drive innovation, improve customer experiences, and streamline operations.

Remote and Hybrid Leadership

The COVID-19 pandemic accelerated the adoption of remote work and hybrid models. In the future, leaders will need to excel in managing remote teams, fostering collaboration across distances, and creating inclusive work cultures that transcend physical boundaries.

Emphasis on Emotional Intelligence

Emotional intelligence (EQ) is gaining prominence in leadership. Leaders with high EQ can navigate complex interpersonal dynamics, build strong relationships, and lead with empathy. EQ will be a critical skill for effective leadership in the future.

Sustainability and Social Responsibility

The future of leadership is increasingly focused on sustainability and social responsibility. Leaders are expected to consider the environmental and societal impact of their decisions and lead departments that prioritise sustainability and ethical practices.

Diversity, Equity, and Inclusion (DEI)

DEI initiatives are reshaping leadership. In the future, leaders will be expected to champion diversity and inclusion, create equitable workplaces, and drive cultural change that fosters belonging and representation.

Agile and Adaptive Leadership

The pace of change is accelerating. Leaders of the future must be agile and adaptive, able to pivot quickly in response to shifting market dynamics, technological advancements, and unforeseen challenges.

Data-Driven Decision-Making

Data-driven leadership is on the rise. Leaders who can harness data analytics to inform decisions, predict trends, and drive innovation will have a competitive edge.

Collaboration Across Boundaries

The future of leadership will involve collaboration not only within departments but also across organisational boundaries. Leaders will need to build partnerships, ecosystems, and networks to solve complex challenges.

Lifelong Learning and Reskilling

Leadership is a journey of continuous learning. In the future, leaders will need to embrace lifelong learning and reskilling to stay relevant in a rapidly changing business landscape.

Crisis Preparedness

The COVID-19 pandemic highlighted the importance of crisis preparedness. Leaders of the future will need to proactively plan for crises, build resilience into their departments, and be ready to lead through adversity.

Purpose-Driven Leadership

Purpose-driven leadership is gaining traction. Leaders who can articulate a compelling purpose, align their departments with it, and inspire a sense of meaning and mission will attract and retain top talent.

Cross-Cultural Leadership

As businesses expand globally, cross-cultural leadership is essential. Leaders must understand and navigate diverse cultural norms, communication styles, and business practices.

Technological Integration

The integration of technology into leadership will continue to evolve. Leaders may need to work alongside AI-powered tools, automation, and virtual assistants, which can enhance decision-making and productivity.

Personal Branding and Thought Leadership

Leaders of the future will be expected to establish personal brands and thought leadership. Building a strong online presence and sharing insights through content creation will be valuable for departmental leaders.

Adaptive Strategies

In a volatile business environment, leaders must develop adaptive strategies that are flexible and responsive to change. Traditional, rigid strategic plans may become less relevant.

Mental Health and Wellbeing

Leaders will increasingly prioritise the mental health and wellbeing of their teams. Creating a supportive work environment and addressing burnout will be key concerns.

Global Leadership Mindset

Leaders must adopt a global leadership mindset, considering the interconnectedness of markets, economies, and supply chains. Geopolitical awareness and international business acumen are valuable skills.

Blockchain and Cybersecurity Leadership

With the rise of blockchain technology and cybersecurity threats, leaders will need to understand and navigate these domains to protect their departments from data breaches and ensure secure transactions.

Innovative Leadership Models

Leadership models are evolving. Some organisations are experimenting with non-hierarchical structures, distributed leadership, and shared leadership models that emphasise collaboration and shared responsibility.

Responsible AI and Ethics

As AI becomes more integrated into business processes, leaders must address ethical concerns and ensure responsible AI usage that aligns with societal values.

THE TAKEAWAY: The Future Leader's Journey

The future leadership is a dynamic landscape shaped by a myriad of trends and insights. Leaders who embrace change, cultivate new skills, and navigate emerging challenges will be well-prepared to lead their departments to success in the evolving business landscape. The future leader's journey is not a destination but a continuous exploration of possibilities, growth, and adaptability in an ever-changing world.

LEADERSHIP VALUES

What are yours?

Values are the foundational principles that shape our beliefs, guide our actions, and define who we are as individuals and as members of a collective, such as a family, community, or organisation. They serve as a moral compass, influencing the decisions we make and the relationships we form. In the context of leadership, values take on even greater significance, as they play a central role in shaping the character and effectiveness of leaders.

Integrity: Leaders must be honest and trustworthy. They should adhere to a strong moral and ethical code, consistently doing what is right even when it's difficult.

Respect: Leaders should treat all individuals with respect, regardless of their background, position, or beliefs. This includes actively listening to others and valuing their contributions.

Accountability: Good leaders take responsibility for their actions and decisions. They don't blame others but instead own up to their mistakes and work to rectify them.

Empathy: Empathetic leaders understand and care about the emotions and needs of their team members. They can relate to their experiences and provide support when necessary.

Courage: Leadership often requires making tough decisions and taking calculated risks. Courageous leaders stand up for their convictions and face challenges head-on.

Vision: Leaders should have a clear and inspiring vision for the future. They communicate this vision to their team and work towards its realisation.

Humility: Humble leaders recognise that they don't have all the answers and are open to learning from others. They don't let their ego get in the way of collaboration and growth.

Teamwork: Effective leaders promote a sense of unity and collaboration within their teams. They understand the value of diverse perspectives and foster an inclusive environment.

Innovation: Leaders encourage creativity and innovation, both in themselves and their teams. They are open to new ideas and are willing to experiment.

Decisiveness: Leaders must make decisions, often with limited information. They do so in a timely manner and are willing to adjust course if needed.

Communication: Strong communication skills are essential for leaders. They should be able to articulate their thoughts clearly and listen actively to others.

Adaptability: In a constantly changing world, leaders need to be adaptable and flexible. They can adjust their strategies and plans in response to new challenges and opportunities.

Patience: Patience is important, especially in dealing with setbacks and in developing the skills of team members. Leaders understand that growth and progress take time.

Service: Servant leadership involves prioritizing the needs of others and serving the greater good. Leaders who put the well-being of their team and organisation first often find long-term success.

Transparency: Leaders are open and transparent in their actions and decision-making. They share information and reasons behind their choices, building trust within the team.

Consistency: Leaders are reliable and consistent in their behaviour and decision-making, which helps create a stable and predictable work environment.

Fairness: Fair leaders treat everyone equitably and impartially. They don't show favouritism and base their decisions on merit and objective criteria.

Responsiveness: Good leaders are attentive to the needs and concerns of their team members and stakeholders. They take action to address issues promptly.

Passion: Passionate leaders are enthusiastic about their work and inspire others with their energy and dedication.

Ethical Decision-Making: Leaders make ethical choices, even when it's challenging. They consider the impact of their decisions on all stakeholders and adhere to a strong code of ethics.

READING LIST

"Leadership and Self-Deception" by The Arbinger Institute (2000)

"Leadership from the Inside Out" by Kevin Cashman (2000)

"Primal Leadership" by Daniel Goleman, Richard Boyatzis, and Annie McKee (2002)

"Leaders Eat Last" by Simon Sinek (2014)

"Leadership BS: Fixing Workplaces and Careers One Truth at a Time" by Jeffrey Pfeffer (2015)

"Leadership in War" by Andrew Roberts (2019)

"Start with Why" by Simon Sinek (2009)

"Leadership on the Line" by Ronald A. Heifetz and Marty Linksy (2002)

"Tribal Leadership" by Dave Logan, John King, and Hale Fischer-Wright (2008)

"The Leadership Pipeline" by Ram Charam, Stephen Dotter, and James Noel (2000)

"Turn the Ship Around!" by L. David Marquette (2012)

"The Lean Start-up" by Eric Rise (2011)

"Drive: The Surprising Truth About What Motivates Us" by Daniel H. Pink (2009)

"The Art of Possibility" by Rosamunde Stone Zander and Benjamin Zander (2000)

"The 21 Irrefutable Laws of Leadership" by John C. Maxwell (2007)

"Leadership 2.0" by Travis Bradberry and Jean Greaves (2009)

"The Five Dysfunctions of a Team" by Patrick Lencioni (2002)

"The Leadership Challenge" by James M. Kouzes and Barry Z. Posner (2002)

"Mindset: The New Psychology of Success" by Carol S. Dweck (2006)

"The No Asshole Rule" by Robert I. Sutton (2007)

"Dare to Lead" by Breen Brown (2018)

"Leaders: Strategies for Taking Charge" by Warren Bennis and Burt Nanus (2003)

"The Speed of Trust" by Stephen M.R. Covey (2006)

"Leadership and the New Science" by Margaret J. Wheatley (2006)

"Leadership in a Time of Crisis" by Andrew J. Durbin (2002)

"The Leadership Moment" by Michael Useem (2008)

"The Advantage" by Patrick Lencioni (2012)

"Leadership in War" by Andrew Roberts (2019)

"The Leadership Gap" by Lolly Discal (2017)

"The Lean Manager" by Michael Bale and Daniel T. Jones (2005)

"Leadership That Gets Results" by Daniel Goleman (2000)

"Leadership Without Easy Answers" by Ronald A. Heifetz (1998)

"Leadership and the One Minute Manager" by Ken Blanchard, Patricia Nigari, and Dread Zigarmi (1985)

"Leadership 3.0" by Brad Limerick (2015)

"Drive: The Surprising Truth About What Motivates Us" by Daniel H. Pink (2009)

"The Culture Code" by Daniel Coyle (2018)

"Primal Leadership" by Daniel Goleman, Richard Boyatzis, and Annie McKee (2002)

"The Power of Full Engagement" by Jim Loehr and Tony Schwartz (2003)

"The Leadership Handbook" by John C. Maxwell (2018)

"The Innovator's Dilemma" by Clayton Christensen (1997)

As we reach the conclusion of this book on leadership, I want to leave you with an encouraging message that encapsulates the essence of our journey together.

Leadership is not a destination; it's a continuous journey of growth and self-discovery. Throughout this book, we've explored various aspects of leadership, drawing inspiration from a diverse cast of leaders and visionaries. We've examined the importance of vision, empathy, communication, vulnerability, and resilience, among other qualities.

What I hope you've found in these pages are insights and perspectives that resonate with your own leadership journey. Perhaps you've identified strengths you already possess, areas where you excel, and principles that align with your values and aspirations as a leader. I encourage you to embrace and nurture these strengths, for they are the building blocks of your leadership identity.

Equally important, you may have encountered ideas or practices that challenge your current approach to leadership. These points might have sparked a desire to re-evaluate, refine, or even completely transform certain aspects of your leadership style. This willingness to question and adapt is a hallmark of growth-oriented leadership.

As you reflect on the content of this book, I encourage you to do so with an open mind and a sense of curiosity. Select the principles and insights that resonate most with you, those that you feel will have the greatest impact on your leadership journey. Consider how you can integrate them into your daily practices and interactions.

Simultaneously, do not shy away from the areas where you wish to improve or revisit. Recognize that leadership growth often involves acknowledging vulnerabilities and areas for development. This willingness to confront your own challenges and engage in self-improvement is a sign of true leadership maturity.

Remember that leadership is not a solitary endeavour. It thrives in the context of relationships and collaboration. Seek out mentors, peers, and trusted advisors who can support your growth and provide valuable insights. Engage in meaningful dialogue and exchange ideas with others who share your passion for leadership excellence.

Above all, embrace the idea that leadership is a journey without a fixed endpoint. It's a continuous process of learning, adapting, and evolving. The most effective leaders are those who remain humble and receptive to new perspectives, even as they inspire and guide others.

So, as you embark on your ongoing leadership journey, carry with you the insights and inspiration you've gathered from this book. Let them serve as guideposts on your path to becoming the leader you aspire to be. Remember that leadership is not about perfection; it's about progress, and the journey is as valuable as the destination.

I encourage you to take deliberate steps towards your leadership goals, celebrate your successes, learn from your setbacks, and, above all, enjoy the profound and rewarding adventure that is leadership. Your impact as a leader extends far beyond yourself; it touches the lives of those you lead and the communities you serve.

Thank you for joining me on this exploration of leadership. I have every confidence that your journey will be marked by growth, impact, and the fulfilment that comes from inspiring and empowering others.

With warm regards,

Terry x

www.ingramcontent.com/pod-product-compliance
Lightning Source LLC
Chambersburg PA
CBHW072206290526
45794CB00004B/1678